Prepared in cooperation with Hawaiʻi Cooperative Studies Unit, University of Hawaiʻi Hilo

Abundance, Distribution, and Population Trends of the Iconic Hawaiian Honeycreeper, the ʻIʻiwi (*Vestiaria coccinea*) throughout the Hawaiian Islands

Open-File Report 2013–1150

U.S. Department of the Interior
U.S. Geological Survey

U.S. Department of the Interior
SALLY JEWELL, Secretary

U.S. Geological Survey
Suzette M. Kimball, Acting Director

U.S. Geological Survey, Reston, Virginia: 2013

For more information on the USGS—the Federal source for science about the Earth, its natural and living resources, natural hazards, and the environment—visit *http://www.usgs.gov* or call 1–888–ASK–USGS

For an overview of USGS information products, including maps, imagery, and publications, visit *http://www.usgs.gov/pubprod*

To order this and other USGS information products, visit *http://store.usgs.gov*

Suggested citation:
Paxton, E.H., Gorresen, P.M., and Camp, R.J., 2013, Abundance, distribution, and population trends of the iconic Hawaiian Honeycreeper, the 'I'iwi (*Vestiaria coccinea*) throughout the Hawaiian Islands: U.S. Geological Survey Open-File Report 2013-1150, 59 p.

Figures

Tables

Contents

Abundance, Distribution, and Population Trends of the Iconic Hawaiian Honeycreeper, the ʻIʻiwi (*Vestiaria coccinea*) throughout the Hawaiian Islands

By Eben H. Paxton[1], P. Marcos Gorresen[2], and Richard J. Camp[2]

[1] U.S. Geological Survey Pacific Island Ecosystems Research Center
[2] Hawaiʻi Cooperative Studies Unit, University of Hawaiʻi at Hilo

Abstract

Naturalists in the 1800s described the ʻIʻiwi (*Vestiaria coccinea*) as one of the most abundant forest birds, detected in forested areas from sea level to tree line across all the major Hawaiian Islands. However, in the late 1800s, ʻIʻiwi began to disappear from low elevation forests, and by the mid-1900s, the species was largely absent from low- and mid-elevation areas. Today, ʻIʻiwi are restricted to high-elevation forests on the islands of Hawaiʻi, east Maui, and Kauaʻi, with a few birds apparently persisting on Oʻahu, Molokaʻi, and west Maui. ʻIʻiwi are highly vulnerable to introduced disease, and the prevalence of avian malaria in low and mid-elevations is believed to be the cause of ʻIʻiwi being restricted to high elevations where temperatures are too cold for the development of the disease and its mosquito vector. With global warming, it is feared that the disease will move quickly into the high-elevation forests where the last ʻIʻiwi reside, threatening their viability. The U.S. Fish and Wildlife Service was petitioned to list the ʻIʻiwi as an Endangered Species in 2010, and this report provides a comprehensive review of the abundance, distribution, and trends using historical survey data as well as the most recently available survey information (up to 2012). We estimate the total population size of ʻIʻiwi at 550,972–659,864 (mean = 605,418) individuals. Of these, 90 percent are on the island of Hawaiʻi, followed by east Maui (about 10 percent), with less than 1 percent on Kauaʻi. ʻIʻiwi population trends vary across the islands. ʻIʻiwi population in Kauaʻi has experienced sharp declines, with a projected trend of 92 percent decline over a 25 year period based on the 2000–2012 surveys. On East Maui, the northeastern region has experienced declines (34 percent over a 25 year period), while the southeastern region has been stable to moderately increasing. On the island of Hawaiʻi, population trends are mixed. On the windward side, populations are largely declining, although the northern section (Hakalau Forest) has stable populations. On the leeward side, results suggest a strongly increasing population, with estimates of as much as a 147 percent increase over a 25 year period from the Puʻu Waʻawaʻa region. However, it is unclear how much these results from the leeward side of Hawaiʻi show a population trend contrary to population trends in all other areas or are an artifact of a sparsely sampled area. Trends by elevation suggest a large decrease in numbers of ʻIʻiwi at elevations below 1,200 meters on Kauaʻi and northeast Maui. Low elevation ʻIʻiwi populations also appear to have decreased in other regions, although low-elevation areas are not surveyed as often as other areas because of their lack of native forest birds. An exception to this pattern was the lower portions of the Hakalau Forest National Wildlife Refuge Kona Unit in the central leeward part of the island of Hawaiʻi, where populations appeared stable at the lower elevations. Based on the most recent surveys (up to 2012), approximately 50 percent of ʻIʻiwi live in a narrow, 500-meter band at elevations of 1,200–1,700 meters, suggesting that ʻIʻiwi are vulnerable to future shifts in climate.

Introduction

The Hawaiian Islands, one of the world's most remote archipelagos, has experienced high rates of extinctions since the arrival first of Polynesians between 800 and 1,200 years ago and, more recently, with European contact 230 years ago. Seventy-one known species and subspecies of forest birds native to Hawai'i went extinct between the arrival of Polynesian and first contact with Europeans, while another 24 have disappeared since Europeans arrived (Banko and Banko, 2009). Today, of the 21 extant species, 11 are endangered or exist in only captivity. Of the species that became extinct, many vanished after the introduction of disease, but habitat loss, introduced predators and competitors, and invasive plants and animals that have degraded forests have all contributed to bring tremendous change to the Hawaiian Islands (Price and others, 2009).

The 'I'iwi (*Vestiaria coccinea*) is a nectarivorous honeycreeper that currently lives on the five largest islands of Hawai'i, primarily above 1,200 m in elevation in closed-canopied, high-stature forests dominated by 'ōhi'a lehua (*Metrosideros polymorpha*) and koa (*Acacia koa*) trees (Fancy and Ralph, 1998). The 'I'iwi is a visually spectacular bird, with bright red-orange plumage, contrasting black wings and tail with white edging, and a large decurved bill presumed to be adapted to curved flowers such as the once-common lobelioid plants (Campanulaceae) (Fancy and Ralph, 1998). Today, I'iwi primarily subsist on the flowers of the abundant 'ōhi'a tree, supplemented by flowers from other plants and insects. Early naturalists remarked on large flights of 'I'iwi up and down mountain slopes as they sought flowering plants and trees across the landscape. Such movements presumably exposed 'I'iwi to disease when they moved to low elevations, and such large movements have not been noted in recent decades (Hart and others, 2011). However, research conducted in the early 2000s has shown that 'I'iwi do at least occasionally move to low-elevation forests for food (Kuntz, 2008).

Although now restricted mostly to remote, high-elevation forests above 1,200 m, the 'I'iwi was once described by early European visitors as one of the most common species on all the Hawaiian Islands (Banko, 1981). Multiple accounts by early naturalists in the late 1800s described the 'I'iwi as being abundant in all wooded areas from near sea level to tree line (Banko, 1981). However, since the early 1900s, accounts of 'I'iwi have documented a steady decrease in abundance, and steady contraction from low-elevation forests to high-elevation forests (Banko, 1981). By the 1940s, 'I'iwi numbers were greatly reduced, with the species becoming extinct on Lānai and largely absent from Moloka'i (Munro, 1944). In mid-elevations, I'iwi have vanished from many areas since the mid-1900s. They were common in the main visitor area of Hawai'i Volcanoes National Park (elevation 1,200 m) in the 1940s, but had retreated to higher elevation forests (elevation 1,700 m) by the 1970s (Banko, 1981).

The 'I'iwi is highly susceptible to introduced disease (Atkinson and LaPointe, 2009), with studies exposing 'I'iwi to infected mosquitoes documenting near 100 percent fatality (Atkinson and others, 1995). Historically, disease has been absent from high elevations where the temperatures are too cool for mosquitoes and the malaria parasite to develop. However, with global warming, it is feared that the disease will move increasingly upward in elevation and threaten the high-elevation sanctuaries where 'I'iwi are currently residing (Benning and others, 2002; Paxton and others, 2012).

Fears of continued declines in 'I'iwi populations and the susceptibility of the species to alien diseases have driven concern for their long-term viability. In 2011 the U.S. Fish and Wildlife Service was petitioned to list the 'I'iwi as an endangered species under the Endangered Species Act (Center for Biological Diversity, 2010). The purpose of this report is to gather all available survey data from the Hawaiian Islands and to provide the most thorough and up-to-date analysis of abundance, distribution, and population trends across the entire range of the 'I'iwi.

Methods

Bird Surveys in Hawai'i

Between 1976 and 1983, an ambitious effort was made by the U.S. Fish and Wildlife Service to determine species distribution and abundance of all forest birds on the main Hawaiian islands as part of the Hawai'i Forest Bird Survey (HFBS) (Scott and others, 1986). HFBS established a quantitative baseline from which changes in bird populations on Hawai'i, Maui, Lāna'i, Moloka'i, and Kaua'i could be ascertained (Scott and others, 1986), and established set protocols for subsequent bird surveys to ensure their comparability. Since the start of the HFBS and related efforts, more than 600 surveys using point-transect methods have been conducted across the main Hawaiian Islands (Camp and others, 2009). Although there are some issues with directly comparing all the surveys, especially when surveys are completed at different times of the year, these multiple decades of surveys provide a detailed record for understanding trends. These surveys have been archived in the Hawai'i Forest Bird Interagency Database to allow for analysis of distribution and trends across time and space.

Distance-Sampling

A point-transect survey is a type of distance sampling for which the probability of detecting birds is modeled as a function of their distance from an observer and other factors to obtain estimates of the effective area sampled and animal density (Buckland and others, 2001, 2004). Point-transect counts of Hawaiian forest birds were conducted following methods described by Scott and others, (1986). Observers received pre-survey training to calibrate for distance estimation and to learn bird vocalizations, thereby minimizing variability among observers and standardizing for local conditions. Trained and calibrated observers recorded the species and detection type (heard, seen, or both), and estimated the horizontal distance in meters from survey station center point to birds detected during 8-minute counts (or alternatively, 6 minutes on Mauna Kea volcano, island of Hawai'i). Time of sampling and weather conditions (cloud cover, rain, wind, and gust strength) also were recorded, and surveying was halted when conditions hindered the ability to detect birds (wind and gusts greater than 20 kilometers per hour and heavy rain). Birds only flying over or through the survey area were excluded. Detections of male and female birds singing and calling were recorded, although the sex of individuals was not noted. Most of the birds encountered were adults because counts were timed during the breeding season and most juveniles had not yet fledged.

Density Estimation

'I'iwi densities were calculated from point-transect distance sampling data following methods described by Buckland and others (2001, 2004), Camp and others (2009), and Thomas and others (2010). Densities (birds/ha) were calculated using the program Distance 6.0, release 2 (Thomas and others, 2010). Observations from all surveys conducted between December and August were pooled to calculate global detection functions by region or island. Stations usually were counted only once during an annual survey; however, when stations were counted more than once, the survey effort was adjusted by the number of times the station was counted. All data were treated as exact measures and modeled accordingly. Candidate models for the detection function were restricted to half normal and hazard-rate detection functions with expansion series of two orders, as recommended by Buckland and others (2001, p. 361 and 365). To improve model precision, the following variables were examined as potential model covariates: observer, time of day, cloud cover, rain, wind, gust strength, year, elevation, precipitation, vegetation class, and detection type. All covariates were treated as a factor, except time of day was treated as a continuous covariate, and year was treated both as a factor and a continuous covariate. Assessing time of day and year as a continuous covariate allowed us to determine if the detection rate varied across time. Data were truncated at a distance where detection probability was less than 10 percent. This procedure facilitates modeling by deleting outliers and reducing the number of parameters needed to modify the detection function. The model selected was that with the lowest second-order Akaike's Information Criterion corrected for small sample sizes (AICc) (Burnham and Anderson, 2002). Candidate model and rankings are presented in appendix A, and final models and associated effective detection radius (EDR) values are presented in appendix B. Survey-specific densities were estimated by applying the global detection function, and variances and confidence intervals (CIs) were derived by bootstrap methods in Distance from 999 iterations (Thomas and others, 2010).

The distance at which birds can be detected depends partly on bird abundance. In our experience, counts of gregarious and highly vocal and mobile birds such as 'I'iwi are more challenging where abundance is high. This is largely attributable to the difficulty of mentally tracking numerous moving individuals and hearing distant birds over the vocalizations of birds nearer to the observer. An additional complication to modeling detectability is that most of the survey data collected after the HFBS for the island of Hawai'i has been collected from a few limited areas with relatively high bird densities (for example, Hakalau Forest National Wildlife Refuge). The available samples are not spatially balanced to produce a global EDR applicable to the species range across high and low densities. To address this issue, we used only HFBS data to model detection functions and to calculate effective detection radii for surveys on the island of Hawai'i. Unlike with most subsequent surveys, the HFBS data were collected across almost the entire species range and closely matched the island wide spatial scale at which EDRs were applied in this study. Additionally, the HFBS was done primarily in June and July, a post-breeding period when 'I'iwi are dispersed across a larger area (Simon and others, 2002). As a result of this, the low encounter rate allows birds to be detected at greater distances, and lessens the problem associated with estimating distances in high bird-density areas. Finally, the lower encounter rate of the HFBS counts better approximates the intermediate abundance observed throughout the species range (which includes both low- and high-density areas).

Abundance Estimation

Population size estimates for each island or region were obtained by extrapolating mean bird density for surveyed areas by the area of available habitat within the species range. Species range was determined based on 'I'iwi occurrence records from the most current survey data (2012). Where current survey data were not available, the most recent survey results were used (most within 5 years, 2008–2012). The species range boundary was delineated so as to include all observed occurrences, and in areas not surveyed, the range included areas not directly surveyed but where projected suitable habitat occurred near surveyed areas. Designation of suitable habitat was qualitatively determined based on 'I'iwi presence at other comparable locations within the species' range and was evaluated separately for each island.

Suitable habitat areas for density extrapolations were produced using elevation and vegetation classifications. Elevation was obtained from a 10-m resolution Digital Elevation Model produced by the U.S. Geological Survey for the National Elevation Dataset. For comparability, the same elevation strata intervals (for example, elevations 900–1,100 m, 1,100–1,300 m, and so on) used by Scott and others (1986) were used for estimating density and abundance in this study. Vegetation classifications were obtained from Landfire2, a GIS layer of Hawaiian land cover types (accessed April 15, 2012, at *http://www.landfire.gov/*), and vegetation classes were corroborated with high-resolution multi-spectral aerial photography (Emerge imagery produced by U.S. Department of Agriculture, Natural Resources

Conservation Service). The vegetation types used in this study differed from those of Scott and others (1986) because statewide mapped data that incorporated their land cover classification system were not available for all areas surveyed for birds in more recent years. Limited sampling in some vegetation types required similar classes to be combined for purposes of modeling bird density. Vegetation class recombinations are listed in appendix C.

Density and population abundance were calculated for all habitat strata for which there were bird survey samples. Unsampled strata did not contribute to population abundance estimates, but the areas constituting these strata nevertheless were presented to identify habitats for which inference was not available. Population abundance estimates were derived for elevation and vegetation habitat variables. These two estimates of abundance generally were similar to each other (appendix E). We averaged the two estimates to derive a single number for the overall abundance of a given island or region by taking the mean of the point estimates and the square root of the summed squared standard errors divided by 4, and multiplied by the t-distribution (1.96) for the CIs. Although this approach does not take into account likely covariance between the two estimates (and, therefore, likely underestimates the variance associated around the mean), it provides a way to include information from both stratifications and a single estimate of abundance per island or region. Large uncertainties associated with estimates derived from surveys with few bird detections (generally less than 10 individuals) precluded the calculation of 'I'iwi abundance for many island and island regions (specifically O'ahu, Moloka'i, west Maui, and Mauna Kea on the island of Hawai'i); these estimates were not used in the overall abundance estimates. Additionally, we excluded other areas where 'I'iwi are believed to occur but no recent surveys have been completed (for example, Kohala Mountains on Hawai'i, Kula Forest Reserve on Maui).

Assessment of Trends in Population Abundance and Species Range

Detecting and interpreting trends in bird populations is an important component of evaluating the conservation status of species. However, such assessments can be sensitive to shifts in sampling effort and location over time. To address this issue, we delineated consistently sampled areas (CSAs) that coincided spatially across time and that were used for subsetting comparable annual survey data. The requirement for spatial consistency was balanced against the need to include as much survey data as possible and to maximize the temporal resolution of the trend analyses. Nevertheless, in some cases, it was necessary to exclude surveys that did not fully extend across a CSA. For example, trend analyses for Kaua'i required delineation of a pair of nested CSAs that spanned overlapping time periods (fig. 1). To maintain the longest time series possible, the data for seven surveys (1989–2012) were subset based the extent of area first surveyed with distance-sampling methods in 1981, resulting in a smaller area but longer time series. In contrast, to produce a time series for the largest possible area and to better match the extent of the species range, a larger CSA was delineated based on the area sampled in 2000 and in four follow-up surveys. CSAs for the islands of Maui and Hawai'i are shown in figures 1 and 2.

Although the HFBS data were spatially balanced samples from which to calculate effective detection radii, the bias inherent in comparing abundance derived from surveys at different times of year meant that these samples could not be included in some analyses of density trends. On Kaua'i, the HFBS and post-HFBS ("subsequent") surveys were conducted during the same months (February–May), and the use of HFBS data from 1981 as a baseline was appropriate for assessing population trends. However, on Maui and Hawai'i, the HFBS was conducted during mid-to-late summer, whereas subsequent surveys were conducted during winter and spring; therefore, the two data sources were not directly comparable. This is especially important because 'I'iwi are known to disperse widely during the non-breeding season. As a result, the first year of the subsequent survey data periods on Maui (1992) and Hawai'i (1986–1999) was used as the baseline for trend assessments with densities determined from

HFBS samples included in trend graphics for reference only. However, HFBS data were used for the quantile regressions (see section, "Trends in Occurrence by Elevation"), where count information was simplified to species presence-absence for a particular elevation. The use of species presence-absence data, versus count data, allows us to evaluate long-term elevational shifts in distribution while minimizing any biases in the counts from different seasons.

Trends in Density

For time series with more than 4 years of surveys we assessed change in 'I'iwi populations by estimating trends with a log-linear regression within a Bayesian framework. Bayesian results generally are more easily interpreted than frequentist tests of the null hypothesis (Camp and others, 2008). More importantly, this approach also permitted us to distinguish negligible or stable trends from statistically inconclusive outcomes. We used a log-linear regression model to calculate the distribution of the posterior probabilities (P) of trend parameters. The proportion of the posterior distribution that was within or outside threshold bounds was assessed in a manner similar to the end-point comparisons; that is, corresponding to a 25-percent change in the population over 25 years. We categorized trends as increasing, decreasing, negligible (that is, stable population), or inconclusive (that is, trend uncertain). The evidence for a particular trend was based on how the distribution of posterior probabilities was apportioned by category, and was interpreted as weak ($P < 0.7$), strong ($0.7 \leq P < 0.9$), or very strong ($P \geq 0.9$). An inconclusive result occurred when variance was high and the posterior distribution gave only weak evidence across the increasing, decreasing, and negligible trend categories.

Log-linear regression was performed with WinBUGS (Lunn and others, 2000; accessed December 1, 2006, at *www.mrc-bsu.cam.ac.uk/bugs.*) in program R (R version 2.15.1; 2012-06-22; R Development Core Team, 2011). The parameter α is the density at time t equals 0 (that is, intercept), β is the rate of change (that is, slope) with each unit increase in time t, and τ equals variance^{-1} (that is, precision). The parameters α and β were given uninformative normal priors, and τ was given an uninformative gamma prior. Year values were centered on a year corresponding to the mid-point of the time series. The model parameters were estimated from 50,000 iterations for each of three chains (that is, model runs) after discarding the first 2,000 iterations (a "burn-in" period). The three chains were pooled (150,000 total samples) to create a posterior distribution. The density per station data were fitted with a traditional least-squares model, with the "lm" command and the "blinreg" function in R used to sample from the joint posterior distribution of beta and sigma following model diagnostics procedures in Maindonald and Braun (2006). Histograms of the simulated posterior draws of the regression coefficients beta and error standard deviation sigma were plotted and inspected visually to detect deviations from a normal distribution. Outliers also were identified using Bayesian residuals and visually inspected. Temporal autocorrelation in annual abundance was assessed with the "acf" function and AIC procedures were used to select the lag autocorrelation that removed serial correlation. For each analysis, there was no evidence that the model residuals differed from a normal distribution (no evidence of skewness or kertosis), and, although there were some outlier points, the trends were conservative in that the variance was greater when they were included rather than excluded. Furthermore, there was no conclusive evidence that an autoregressive model was necessary to control for temporal correlation.

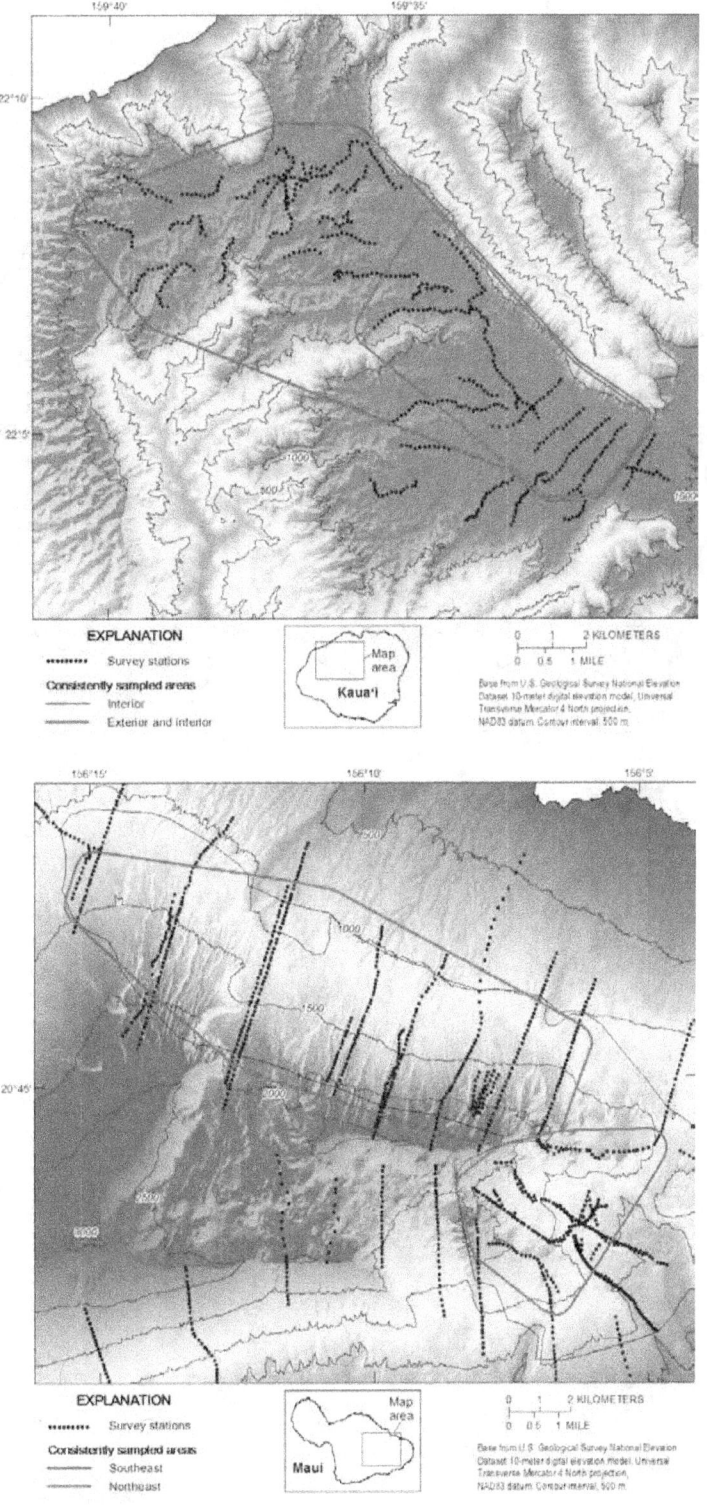

Figure 1. Boundaries of the consistently sampled areas (CSAs) used for assessing trends in density and range decreases of 'I'iwi (*Vestiaria coccinea*) in Kauai and east Maui, Hawai'i. Top panel, Kauai: The blue outline depicts the area surveyed during 1981-2012. The red outline depicts the more extensive areas sampled during 2000–2012. Bottom panel, east Maui: The red outline depicts the northeast CSA and the blue line depicts the southeast CSA.

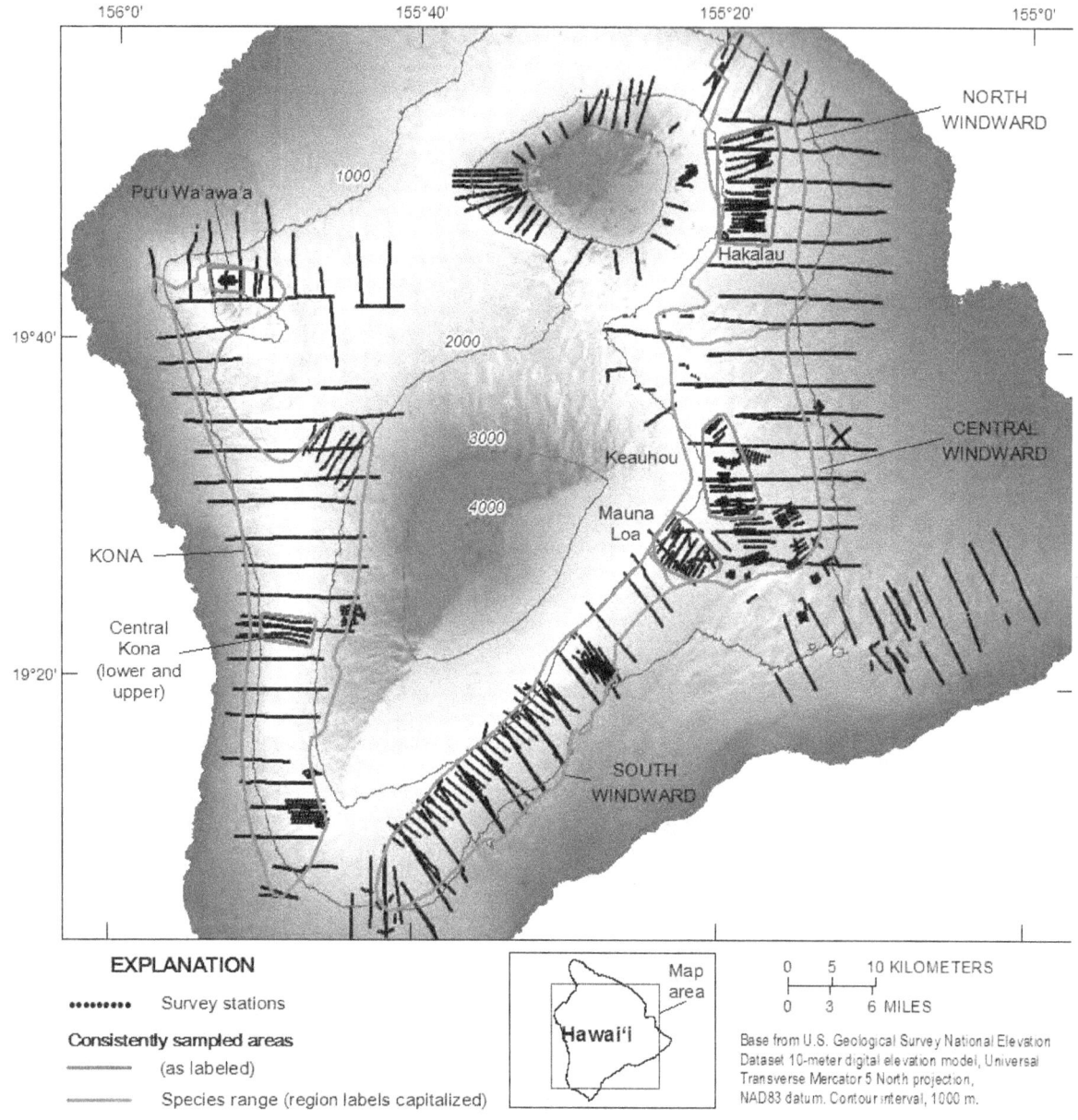

Figure 2. Boundaries of the consistently sampled areas (CSAs). Species range is shown in red, with blue outlines designating the Constantly Surveyed Areas used for assessing trends in density of ʻIʻiwi (*Vestiaria coccinea)* on the island of Hawaiʻi, Hawaiʻi.

Trends in Occurrence by Elevation

Quantile regression was used to determine whether the island-specific distributions of 'I'iwi have decreased by elevation over time. Quantile regression is a method for estimating functional relations between variables for all parts of a probability distribution, and is useful when unequal variation indicates that there is more than a single slope (that is, rate of change) describing the relationship between a response variable and predictor variables (Cade and others, 1999). The method is well suited for examining range decreases as a function of elevation because such patterns are expected to be most pronounced at lower elevations where avian disease and invasive species are most prevalent (Banko and Banko, 2009).

The seasonally dissimilar period during which the HFBS and subsequent surveys were conducted made problematic the use of HFBS-derived densities for trend assessments. However, the HFBS data were still useful for examining trends in 'I'iwi occurrence as a function of elevation. Although the HFBS surveys were conducted when 'I'iwi were highly dispersed, the seasonal effect was expected to be less pronounced for observations treated simply as binary data (that is, detected or not detected) than as measures of abundance.

Linear quantile regression was performed in the statistical program R version 2.15.1 (R Development Core Team, 2011) with the package "quantreg" (Koenker, 2011). Statistical inference for regression coefficients (that is, standard errors, t-statistics, and p-values) were estimated, and CIs were computed by the rank inversion method (Koenker, 2007, 2011). Trends are presented for quantiles 0.05, 0.10, 0.25, 0.50 (median), 0.75, 0.90, and 0.95, which are associated with elevations specific to each region. Decreases in 'I'iwi occurrence with rises in elevation are indicated by positive values for slopes whose 95-percent CI do not bracket zero. To ensure comparability among years, occurrence data were truncated to an elevation range common to all annual survey datasets. For example, data for surveys on northeast Maui were truncated to include only records above 1,000 m for the years 1980, 1992, 2001, 2006, and 2011; a 1996 survey was excluded because all samples for this year were collected above 1,200 m.

Probability of Detecting Small Extant Populations

Estimation of 'I'iwi density and total abundance based on distance sampling was not possible for parts of the species range in which birds were very rare and sparsely distributed. Because 'I'iwi were not detected in the most recent surveys on O'ahu and Moloka'i, we estimated the maximum population size on each island consistent with not being detected given the number of stations surveyed. Therefore, estimates of the population size were based on the extinction inference method proposed by Scott and others, (2008), and calculated as:

$$X = \log \frac{\alpha}{1-p} \qquad (1)$$

where
  X is the maximum possible population size,
  α is the desired level of statistical confidence, and
  p is the ratio of effective area sampled (E) relative to either the range of the species or total survey area (A).

We calculated E as the sum of the effective areas surveyed within A, where the effective area of each station was calculated from the effective detection radius (EDR) from the Kaua'i and Maui distance analyses as $\pi \cdot \text{EDR}^2$.

Results

Range-wide

We estimate the overall abundance of 'I'iwi at 605,418 individuals (95-percent CI = 550,972–659,864)(table 1). Most I'iwi are restricted to high-elevation forests of the island of Hawai'i (90 percent), followed by east Maui (about 10 percent), and Kaua'i (less than 1 percent); only relict populations exist, if at all, on O'ahu, west Maui, and Moloka'i (fig. 3, table 1). Across the islands, an estimated 90 percent of 'I'iwi live in a narrow band at an elevation of 1,300–1,900 m, and mainly in montane forest, with 61 percent in montane wet forest, 35 percent in montane mesic forest, 3 percent in lowland wet-mesic forest, and remaining habitats constituting less than 1 percent of distribution (appendix E).

Table 1. Range size and mean abundance (with 95-percent confidence interval) by islands and region for 'I'iwi (*Vestiaria coccinea*) throughout Hawai'i. The abundance estimates are the mean of estimates derived separately from elevation and vegetation classifications (appendix E), with 95-% CIs calculated as mean abundance plus-or-minus the square root of the summed squared SE divided by 4 times t-distribution (1.96). **Abbreviations:** ha, hectare; %, percent; CI, confidence interval; SE, standard error.

Island/region	Area (ha)	Mean abundance	Lower 95% CI	Upper 95% CI
Kaua'i	5,436	2,551	1,934	3,167
O'ahu		[2]50		
Maui, east	13,201	59,859	54,569	65,148
Maui, west	1,887	[1]176		
Moloka'i	1,800	[1]80		
Hawai'i (all regions)	174,840	543,009	516,312	569,706
Hawai'i, north windward	24,926	277,055	258,075	296,035
Hawai'i, central windward	40,773	71,524	62,662	80,386
Hawai'i, Ka'ū	33,680	28,325	23,138	33,512
Hawai'i, south Kona	12,489	3,489	2,059	4,918
Hawai'i, central Kona	25,441	139,829	124,649	155,009
Hawai'i, north Kona	21,231	22,787	18,444	27,130
Kohala Mountains	5,600	[1]802		
Mauna Kea	4,200	[1]482		
[3] Species total		605,418	550,972	659,864

[1] Estimates from Scott and others (1986) surveys

[2] Estimate from BirdLife International (2012)

[3] Total estimates do not include Scott and others 1986 estimates and O'ahu estimate

Trends vary across the range of the 'I'iwi, with lower elevation parts of their range generally declining, and even most high elevation areas showing evidence of declines (fig. 1, table 2). Central Kona on Hawai'i Island is one area where low elevation populations appear to be stable or increasing, and the entire Kona coast stands out as an area of stable to increasing populations.

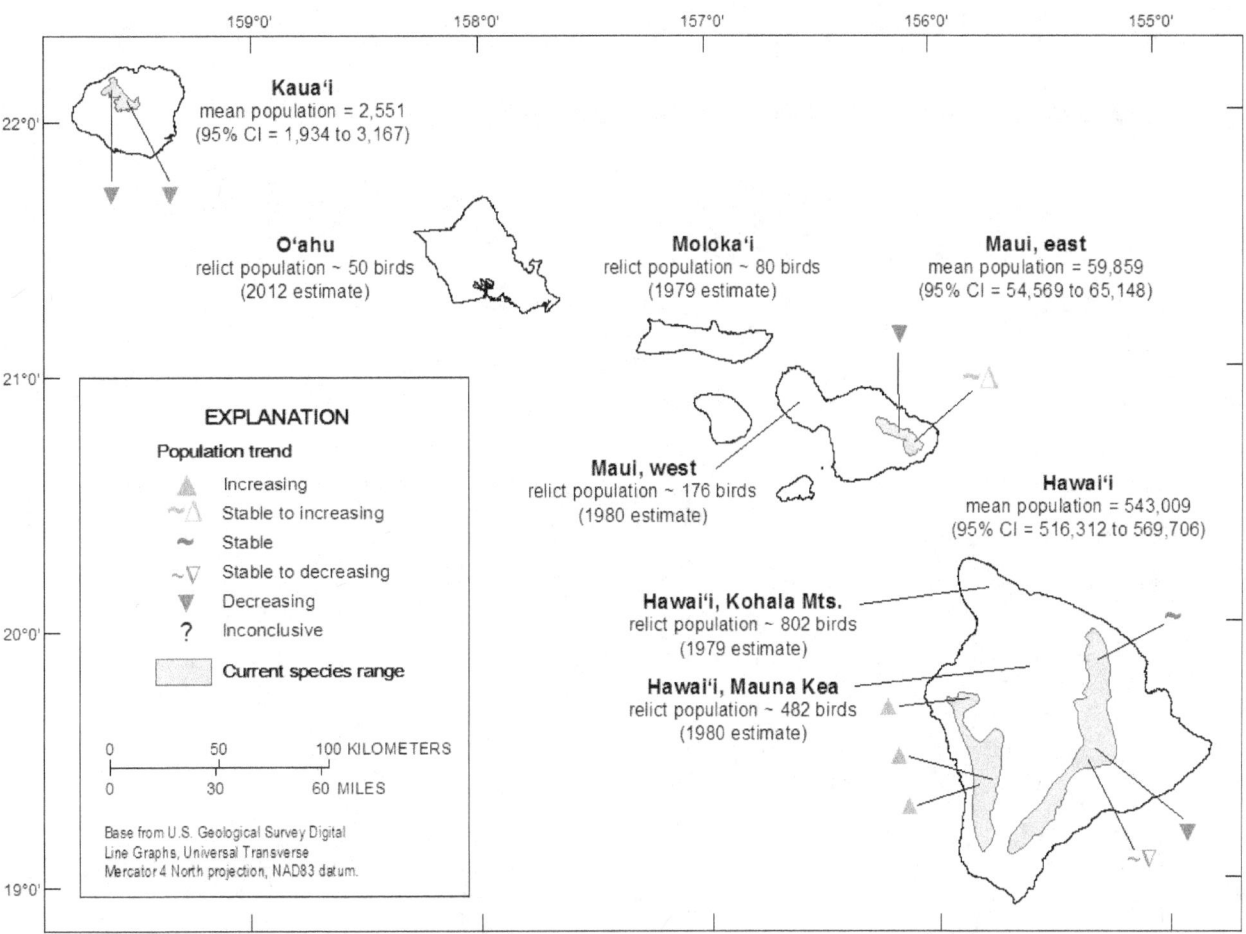

Figure 3. Distribution, mean population size (95-percent confidence interval), and population trends by region for 'I'iwi (*Vestiaria coccinea*) across its range in Hawai'i. See table 1 for mean abundances, and table 2 for details on population trends.

11

Table 2. Trends in 'I'iwi (*Vestiaria coccinea*) density by island, consistently sampled area (CSA; see figs. 1 and 2), and survey period, throughout Hawai'i. The ecological relevance of a trend as estimated by Bayesian log-linear regression was based on a standard metric defined as a 25% change in density over 25 years. The metric corresponds to an annual rate of change with significance defined by a threshold lower bound of $\varphi_l = -0.0119$ and an upper bound of $\varphi_u = 0.0093$. For log-linear regression results, statistics include the slope coefficient ($\hat{\beta}$), standard deviation (SD), and 95% credible interval (CI). The posterior probabilities (P) of the regression slope are assessed for each trend category (declining, negligible, and increasing), where $0.7 < P < 0.9$ indicates strong evidence, and $P > 0.9$ very strong evidence of a trend. Interpretation of an observed trend is summarized as increasing (▲), stable (—), decreasing (▼), stable to increasing ($\sim\triangle$), stable to declining ($\sim\square$), and inconclusive (Inc). Given the observed regression slope, projected trend is a standardized measure of the percent change in population size over a 25-year period.

| Island | CSA | Survey period | $\hat{\beta}$ | SD | 95% CI | Posterior Probability | | | Observed trend | Projected trend (%) |
						Declining $\hat{\beta} < \varphi_l$	Negligible $\varphi_l < \hat{\beta} < \varphi_u$	Increasing $\hat{\beta} > \varphi_u$		
Kaua'i	interior	1981–2012	-0.0406	0.0027	-0.0460 to -0.0354	1.000	0	0	▶	- 63
	interior	2000–2012	-0.0794	0.0127	-0.1048 to -0.0551	1.000	0	0	▶	- 86
	exterior	2000–2012	-0.1384	0.0220	-0.1851 to -0.0989	1.000	0	0	▶	- 97
	both	2000–2012	-0.0996	0.0110	-0.0993 to -0.0786	1.000	0	0	▶	- 92
Maui	northeast	1992–2011	-0.0172	0.0047	-0.0264 to -0.0080	0.868	0.132	0	▶	- 34
	southeast	1992–2012	0.0082	0.0031	0.0021 to 0.0143	0	0.635	0.365	~△	+ 22
Hawai'i	Hakalau	1999–2012	-0.0094	0.0034	-0.0160 to -0.0027	0.226	0.774	0	—	- 20
	Keauhou	1995–2012	-0.0270	0.0033	-0.0334 to -0.0207	1.000	0	0	▶	- 4
	Mauna Loa	1986–2012	-0.0139	0.0104	-0.0356 to 0.0051	0.560	0.433	0.007	~□	- 29
	Central Kona - upper	1995–2012	0.0226	0.0069	0.0091 to 0.0361	0	0.027	0.973	▲	+ 71
	Central Kona - lower	1995–2012	0.0294	0.0130	0.0043 to 0.0553	0.001	0.058	0.941	▲	+ 9
	Pu'u Wa'awa'a	1990–2009	0.0383	0.0163	0.0075 to 0.0719	0.001	0.031	0.967	▲	+ 147

Kauaʻi

The ʻIʻiwi population of Kauaʻi appears to be in rapid decline, with both the species range and population abundance decreasing fast (fig. 4). Early historical records (1887–1902) note the presence of ʻIʻiwi at elevations as low as about 700 m (Banko, 1981), which suggests an expanse of available forest habitat of about 28,000 ha. By the late 1960s to early 1970s, the species was observed only as low as elevations of about 900 m, and delineation of the upland area encompassing the survey sites at which ʻIʻiwi were detected gave a species range of about 16,400 ha (fig. 5). During this time period, the core population in the interior of the Alakaʻi Plateau numbered about 7,800 birds (± 2,300 SE) (Scott and others, 1986). A 1981 survey of the same core population produced an estimate of 5,400 (± 264 SE; Scott and others, 1986). By 2000, the area of the species range had decreased to about 10,064 ha and the island-wide population numbered about 9,985 birds (± 960 SE) (Foster and others, 2004). As of 2012, the total population size of ʻIʻiwi on Kauaʻi was estimated at 1,934–3,167 individuals (mean = 2,551; table 1, appendix E.1), with a distribution limited to a 5,436-ha area and most birds observed within montane wet forest from 1,100 to 1,300 m in elevation (fig. 6, appendix E.1).

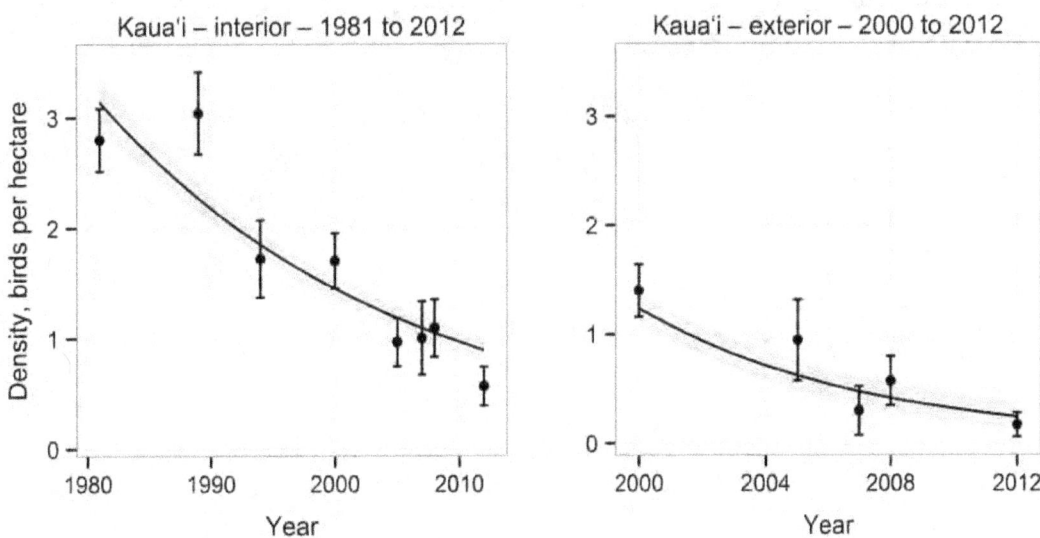

Figure 4.   Trends in ʻIʻiwi (*Vestiaria coccinea*) density (mean birds per hectare at 95-percent confidence interval) on Kauaʻi, Hawaiʻi, for the interior and exterior constantly surveyed areas (fig. 1)(note different survey time periods). The shaded band represents the 95-percent confidence interval of the trend for the entire time series.

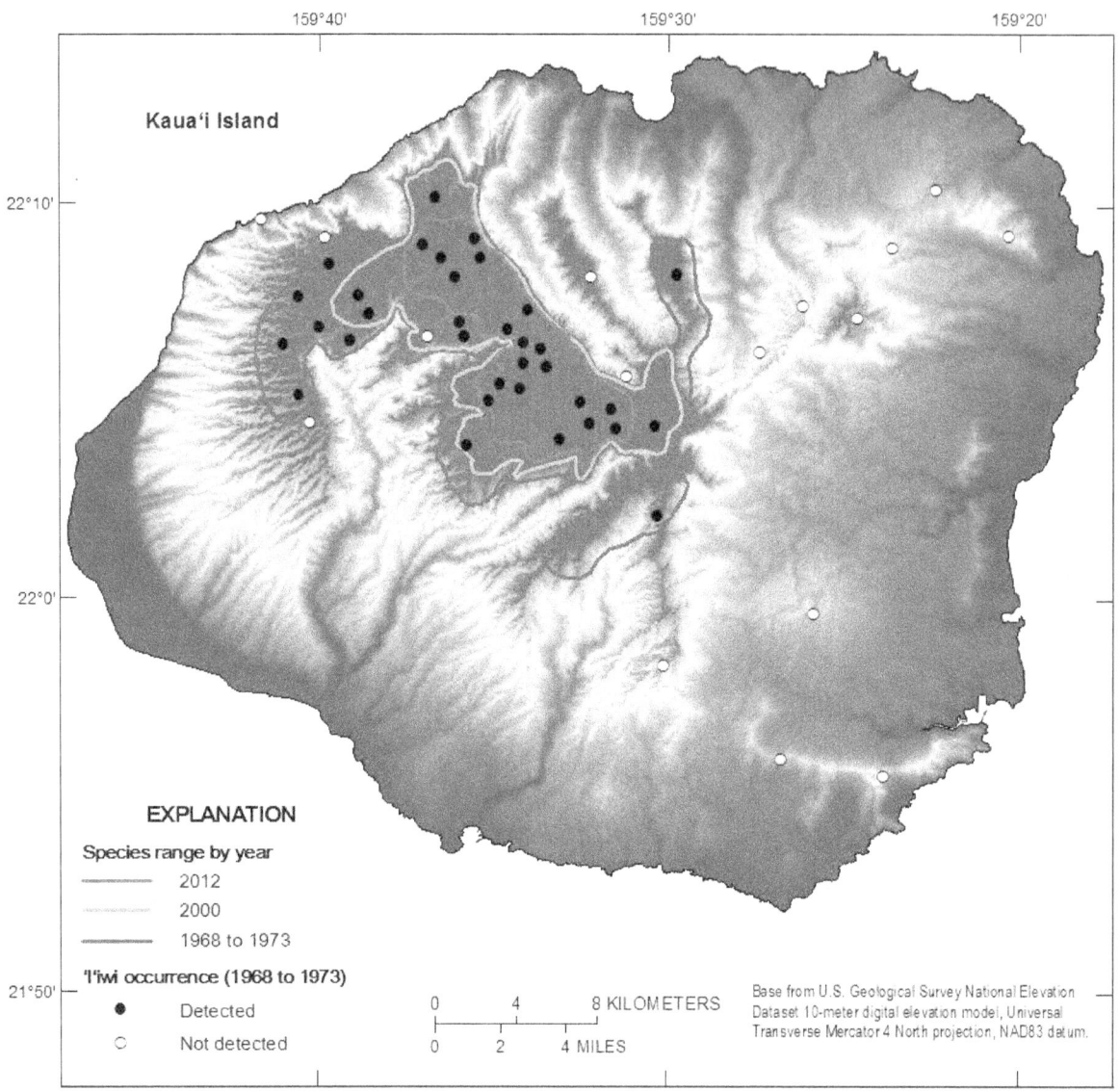

Figure 5.   Extent of 'I'iwi (*Vestiaria coccinea*) species range on Kaua'i, Hawai'i, as determined from surveys completed during 1968–1973 (16,300 hectares; blue outline), 2000 (10,100 hectares; orange outline) and 2012 (5,500 hectares; red outline). Sites for which 'I'iwi were detected (solid circles) and not detected (open circles) are shown for the 1968–1973 survey (source: U.S. Fish and Wildlife Service, 1983). Shading represents elevation from low elevation (browns) to high elevations (greens).

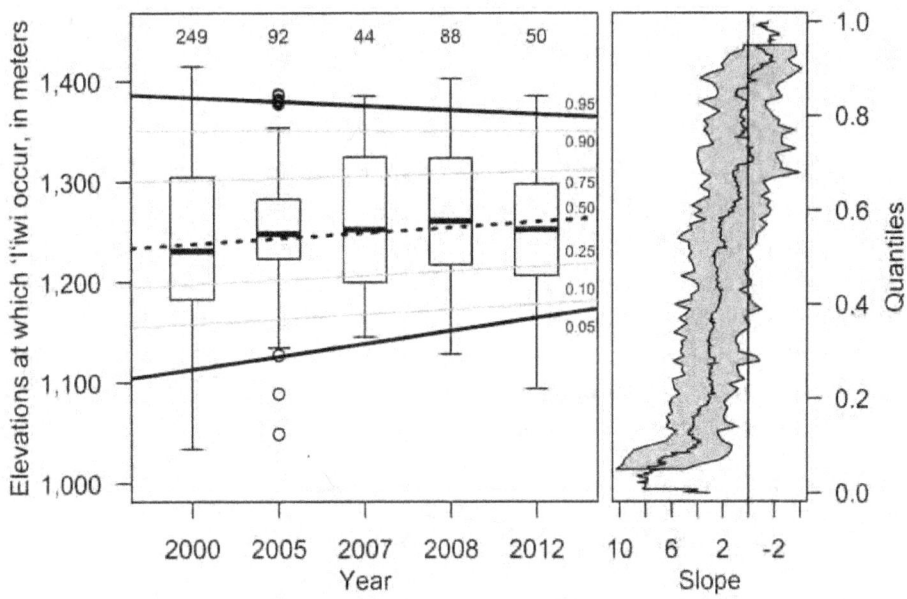

Figure 6. Trends in occurrence of 'I'iwi (*Vestiaria coccinea*) by elevation on Kaua'i, Hawai'i, during 2000–2012, for the combined interior and exterior continuously sampled areas (CSAs). Boxplot (left panel) describes the elevational range per year in 'I'iwi occurrence, and lines depict trends over time at different elevations corresponding to the quantiles of the entire elevational range (0.05, 0.10, 0.25, 0.50, 0.75, 0.90 and 0.95 [linear quantile regression coefficients and statistics are listed in appendix F.1]). Boxplot whiskers denote elevational range within 1.5 times the interquartile range above the 75th percentile and below the 25th percentile, respectively, with outliers beyond the range plotted as individual points. Numbers above boxplot whiskers correspond to sample size (that is, I'iwi occurrence). Upper and lowermost trend lines (corresponding to quantiles 0.05 and 0.95) are shown in black, while the medium elevation (quantile 0.50) is designated as a dotted line. Right panel shows the mean quantile regression slope by elevation (center black line) with 95-percent confidence intervals denoted by gray band. Decreases in 'I'iwi occurrence with rises in elevation are indicated by positive values for slopes whose 95-percent confidence interval does not overlap with zero (vertical thin black line).

Steep declines in 'I'iwi densities are evident from surveys for the CSAs encompassing the Alaka'i Plateau ("interior" and "exterior" CSAs combined, fig. 1). Bird density across the combined regions shows a significant decreasing trend from 2000 to 2012 (slope coefficient [β] = -0.0996 ± 0.0110; 95-percent CI = -0.0993 to -0.0786), which equals a 92 percent reduction in the size of a population over a 25-year period (table 2, fig. 4). The trend is particularly acute for the exterior region ($\hat{\beta}$ = -0.1384 ± 0.0220; 95-percent CI = -0.1851 to -0.0989) with a population size decline of 97 percent over 25 years. The difference in the rates of decline between the 1981–2012 (95-percent CI = -0.0460 to -0.0354) and 2000–2012 (95-percent CI = -0.1048 to -0.0551) survey periods for the interior region indicates that the trend may have accelerated since 2000.

Analysis of 'I'iwi survey detections as a function of elevation (fig. 6) indicates that decreases in the species range on Kaua'i primarily are occurring at the lower elevations of their distributional range. 'I'iwi occurrence below about 1,232 m in elevation has decreased as indicated by significant trends in all quantiles between 0.05 and 0.50 (fig. 6, appendix F.1). The rate of change over the survey period is greatest at the lower elevations, as shown by a mean upward elevation shift of 84 m in bird distribution

(1,082–1,166 m) in the 0.05 quantile. 'I'iwi occurrence at elevations above 1,232 m (that is, in quantiles greater than 0.50) has not changed significantly between 2000 and 2012.

Maui

'I'iwi are distributed as two disjunct populations on Maui, with an east Maui population ranging across 13,201 ha separated from a 1,887-ha area on west Maui by about 30 km of highly altered lowland vegetation. Prior to Western contact, native Hawaiians had converted most lowland forests below 500 m in elevation to an "actively manipulated cultural landscape" (Kirch, 1982), and the area between the east and west Maui populations likely was not a viable habitat for 'I'iwi. Subsequent degradation from a variety of sources (for example, ranching, feral ungulates, and invasive plants; Pratt and Jacobi, 2009) made much of the remnant forest at elevations below 700 m in elevation unsuitable for 'I'iwi by the time the first quantitative bird survey was completed in 1980.

East Maui

Based on survey results for 2011 and 2012, the 'I'iwi population size on east Maui was estimated at 54,569–65,148 individuals (mean = 59,859; table 1, appendix E.2). About two-thirds of the population have been observed in montane wet forest at elevations ranging from 1,100 to 1,900 m (appendixes D.2 and E.2), with the remainder observed in native lowland and introduced forest and montane shrubland at elevations ranging from about 860 to 2,200 m. The current (2012) mean population estimate is about 3 times greater than the estimate of Scott and others (1986; 16,392 ± 1,006 SE). This difference is attributable to the fact that the 1980 HFBS on Maui was done primarily in June and July, a post-breeding period when 'I'iwi are widely dispersed, especially to low elevations and, therefore, are present at low densities in the higher elevation areas primarily surveyed in subsequent years (Simon and others, 2002). Because of this, population estimates and mean density derived from the 1980 HFBS cannot be compared directly with estimates derived from subsequent surveys, which were conducted primarily from March to May. On the other hand, population estimates for east Maui based on 2001 surveys (Camp and others, 2009) were 80 percent higher than the estimates of this study (107,744 'I'iwi in 2001 surveys, versus 59,859 in this study using 2011 and 2012 survey information). This change in population size may be owing partly to declining population sizes, but is also likely an artifact of the variation inherent in surveys, with the 2001 surveys producing some of the highest densities recorded and, therefore, larger population estimates than other years.

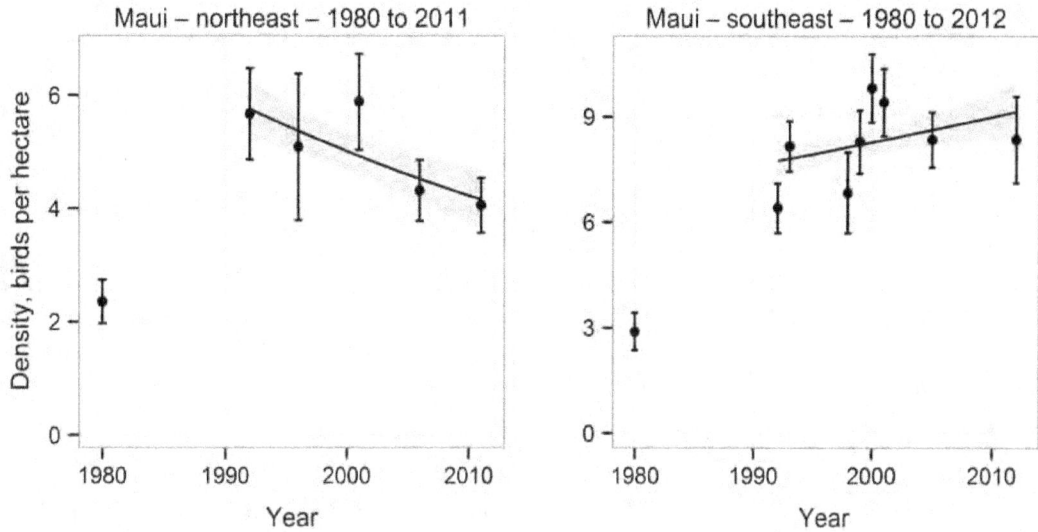

Figure 7. Trends in 'I'iwi (*Vestiaria coccinea*) density (mean birds per hectare and 95-percent confidence interval) on Maui, Hawai'i, within the northeast and southeast constantly surveyed areas (fig. 1). The shaded band represents the 95-percent confidence interval of the trend for the entire time series. Note that the 1980 Hawai'i Forest Bird Survey (HFBS) densities were not included in the trend assessment because of differences in the time of year when the HFBS and all subsequent surveys were conducted.

The I'iwi population showed mixed trends in the two CSAs delineated for east Maui ("northeast" and "southeast"; fig. 1). Bird density in the northeast CSA showed strong evidence of a decline between 1980 and 2011 ($\hat{\beta}$ = -0.0172 ± 0.0047; 95-percent CI = -0.0264 to -0.0080; table 2, fig. 7). This trend in density averages a 34-percent decrease over 25 years. In contrast, densities observed for the southeast CSA from 2000 to 2012 showed a stable to increasing trend ($\hat{\beta}$ = 0.0082 ± 0.0031; 95-percent CI = 0.0021–0.0143)(fig. 7). This trend results in a 22-percent increase in population density over a 25-year period.

The result for the northeast Maui CSA contrasts with that observed for the southeast Maui CSA, in which 'I'iwi occurrence at lower elevations of their distribution (that is, quantiles 0.05–0.50) have not changed significantly between 1980 and 2012 (fig. 8, appendix F.2). However, fewer I'iwi were detected at higher elevations in the southeast Maui CSA over this survey period. 'I'iwi occurrence above about 1,877 m in elevation has decreased, as indicated by significant trends in the 0.75, 0.90 and 0.95 quantiles (fig. 8, appendix F.3). The rate of change was greatest in the upper 25 percent of elevation distribution for southeast Maui CSA as shown by a mean downward shift of 188 m in bird distribution (from 1,877 to 1,689 m) over the 33-year period. The observed increase in bird density in the southeast Maui CSA, coupled with the declines in occurrence at the highest elevations, may indicate different trends in habitat quality between the drier margins of montane forest at higher elevations and wetter forest at mid elevations.

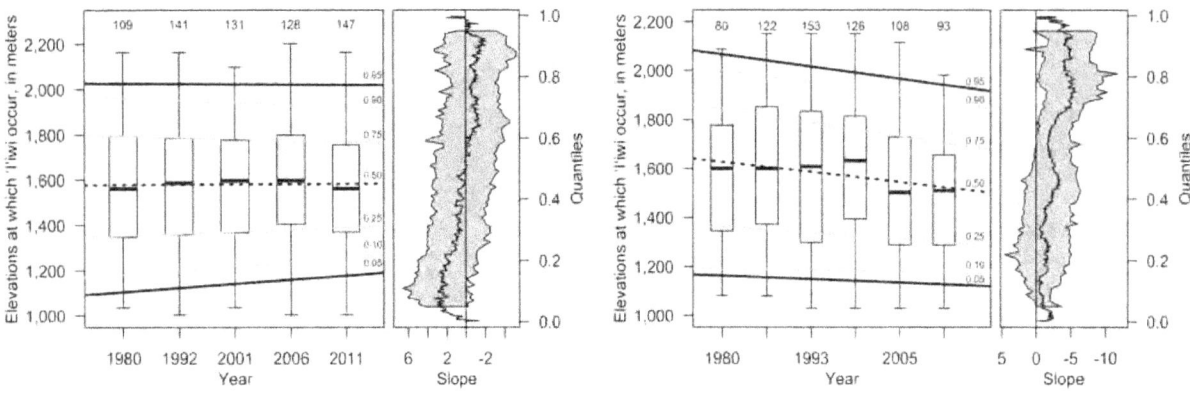

Figure 8. Trends in occurrence of 'I'iwi (*Vestiaria coccinea)* by elevation in the northeast Maui consistently sampled area (CSA) (left panel) and southeast Maui CSA (right panel), Hawai'i. Survey period includes the years 1980, 1992, 2001, 2003, 2005 and 2012 for the northeast Maui CSA, and 1980, 1992, 1996, 2001, 2006, and 2011 for the southeast Maui CSA. See figure 6 for an explanation of graphic features and appendixes F.2 and F.3.

West Maui

The number of 'I'iwi observations on west Maui were not sufficient to model detection functions and to accurately estimate density and population abundance. A total of 5, 2 and 11 'I'iwi were detected in this region in 1980, 1997 and 2010, respectively (fig. 9). The west Maui population in 1980 was estimated at 176 birds (± 74 SE) in an area of about 1,600 ha (Scott and others, 1986). No quantitative inference can be made about the current (2010-2012) population size or distribution.

Oʻahu and Molokaʻi

'Iʻiwi were noted to be in decline on Oʻahu by the early 1900s (Fancy and Ralph, 1998), with increasingly narrower distributions and smaller populations recorded up to the 1970s (Banko, 1981). Shallenberger and Vaughn (1978) noted during 1971–1977 surveys that 'Iʻiwi were observed at elevations above about 427 m. 'Iʻiwi were not detected during an island-wide survey in 1991 (Conry, 1991), although surveys in 1995 and 1996 recorded small numbers of individuals in the north-central Koʻolau Mountains (VanderWerf and Rohrer, 1996). Christmas Bird Count surveys made in the leeward Koʻolau Mountains last observed 'Iʻiwi in 2001 and 2002 (a single bird in each year; National Audubon Society, 2002), and in 2013(John Vetter, personal commun., 2012). The sighting of a juvenile 'Iʻiwi in the south Waiʻanae Mountains in 2008 (E.A. VanderWerf, personal commun., 2012) indicates that either local breeding persists on Oʻahu or interisland movement occurs.

Estimates of the probability of persistence of a small relict 'Iʻiwi population on Oʻahu were produced for a range of values representing remnant population sizes and statistical confidence. Given the absence of sightings on Oʻahu in 1991, the 1991 sampling effort (191 stations at elevations above 427 m), and the average effective detection radius (35.5 m) observed for Iʻiwi on the neighboring islands of Kauaʻi and Maui, there is a 95-percent probability that the 1991 Oʻahu population was less than 922 individuals. That is, at least one individual would likely have been sighted given a population of 922 or more birds. These large values reflect the fact that, despite the 1991 survey having been the most extensive on Oʻahu to date, only about 0.3 percent of the available area above an elevation of 427 m was sampled for 'Iʻiwi. Broader survey coverage might have reduced the estimates of maximum population size. The 'Iʻiwi population on Oʻahu was recently estimated to number less than 50 birds by BirdLife International (2012).

For much of the 20th century, only a remnant population was believed to persist on Molokaʻi. Twelve 'Iʻiwi were detected during the 1979 HFBS of Molokaʻi, and based on these results, Scott and others (1986) estimated 80 ± 33 birds distributed at low densities on the Kamakou Range and Olokuʻi Plateau (fig. 9, top panel). However, surveys between 1988 and 2010 detected very few birds (most recently, 3 individuals in 2004; Camp and others, 2009). Given the absence of detections on Molokaʻi in 2010 and the 2010 sampling effort (97 stations within an 18 km^2 area as the estimated extent of the species range by Scott and others, 1986), there is a 95-percent probability that there were less than 141 birds.

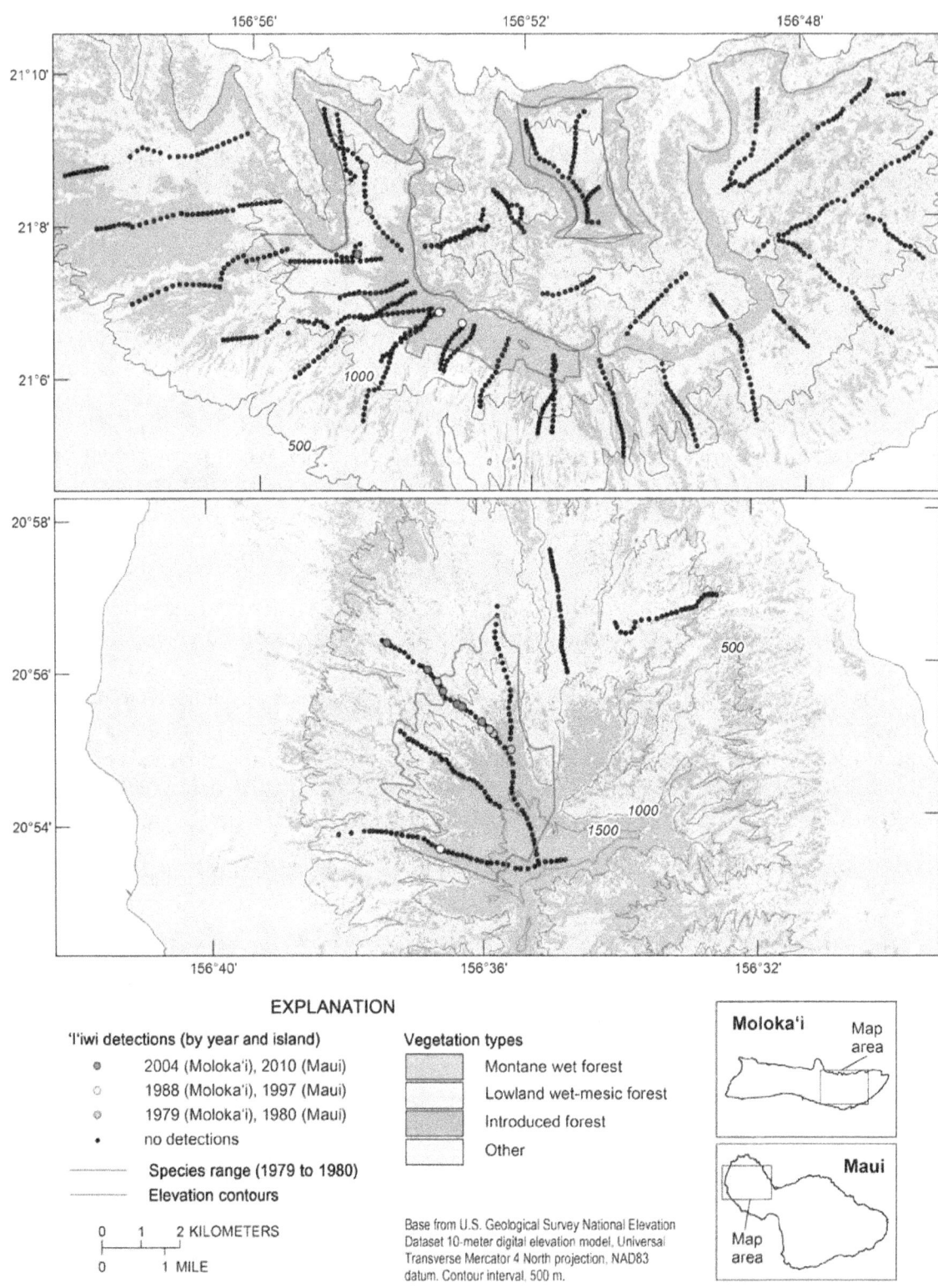

Figure 9. 'I'iwi (*Vestiaria coccinea*) distribution on Moloka'i (top panel) and west Maui (bottom panel), Hawai'i, based on most recent surveys (2004 for Moloka'i, 2010 for west Maui).

Hawai'i

'I'iwi are distributed on both the windward and leeward sides of the island of Hawai'i. With the possible exception of a population on Kohala Mountain, 'I'iwi occur as a single relatively contiguous population throughout the island (Scott and others, 1986; Fancy and Ralph, 1998). However, land cover unsuitable for territorial birds separates areas of occupied forest habitat in many parts of the species range and makes for a disjunct distribution. For the purposes of this study, the species range was delineated to encompass an area of 175,097 ha and to include only the following regions: north windward, central windward, Ka'u, and Kona (fig. 2). Excluded from the range were regions of about 5,600 ha on Kohala Mountain and 4,200 ha on Mauna Kea volcano (as estimated by Scott and others, 1986). The Kohala region was last surveyed in 1979 and only 10 'I'iwi were detected there during the initial visit. The population at that time was estimated at 802 birds (± 286 SE) (Scott and others, 1986). No information is available on the occurrence or abundance of 'I'iwi in the Kohala region since 1979, although they are believed to persist there.

'I'iwi abundance on Mauna Kea is related to māmane tree (*Sophora chrysophylla*) flower bloom (Hess and others, 2001), and most 'I'iwi on Mauna Kea may be visiting temporarily for flower resources. However, a small number of birds may be resident in subalpine woodland, but the delineation of a range boundary reflecting current (~2012) distribution is difficult given that only a few widely dispersed 'I'iwi were detected during (2008-2012) surveys. For example, 'I'iwi decreased from 0.039 birds per station (bps) in the 1998–2002 survey period, to 0.007 bps in the 2003–2007 survey period, and to 0.002 bps in the 2008–2012 survey period. 'I'iwi are sparsely distributed across southwest Mauna Kea based on recent surveys (2008-2012)(appendix D.3).

The island of Hawai'i currently (2012) supports an estimated population of 516,312–569,706 birds (mean = 543,009; table 1, appendix E.3). The mean estimate is about 56 percent greater than the 340,000 birds estimated by Scott and others (1986). As with the surveys on Maui, the 1976–1979 HFBS was conducted primarily during June and July, a post-breeding period in which 'I'iwi densities typically are lower than during the breeding season owing to dispersal to low elevations (Ralph and Fancy, 1994; Hart and others, 2011). Therefore, densities estimated for the HFBS are not directly comparable to those of subsequent surveys that were conducted in the spring during the breeding season.

North Windward (Hakalau)

The windward area of the island of Hawai'i was divided into north and central regions to account for local differences in 'I'iwi densities and to improve regional population size estimates. The north windward region encompasses a 24,926-ha area with 258,075–296,035 birds (mean = 277,055; table 1, appendix E), based on the densities observed in 2012. Density in the 1,700–1,900-m elevation range was estimated at 13.9–18.4 birds per ha (mean = 16.1 ± 1.1 SE), constituting the highest values recorded for 'I'iwi across its range. Although sampling in the region was concentrated at upper elevations, with no sampling within the 4,900 ha of lowland wet-mesic forest below 1,400 m (appendixes D.4 and E.4), recent surveys of this habitat type in the adjacent central windward region did not detect 'I'iwi. Therefore, the unsampled strata is not expected to contribute appreciably to the resulting population estimate for the north windward region.

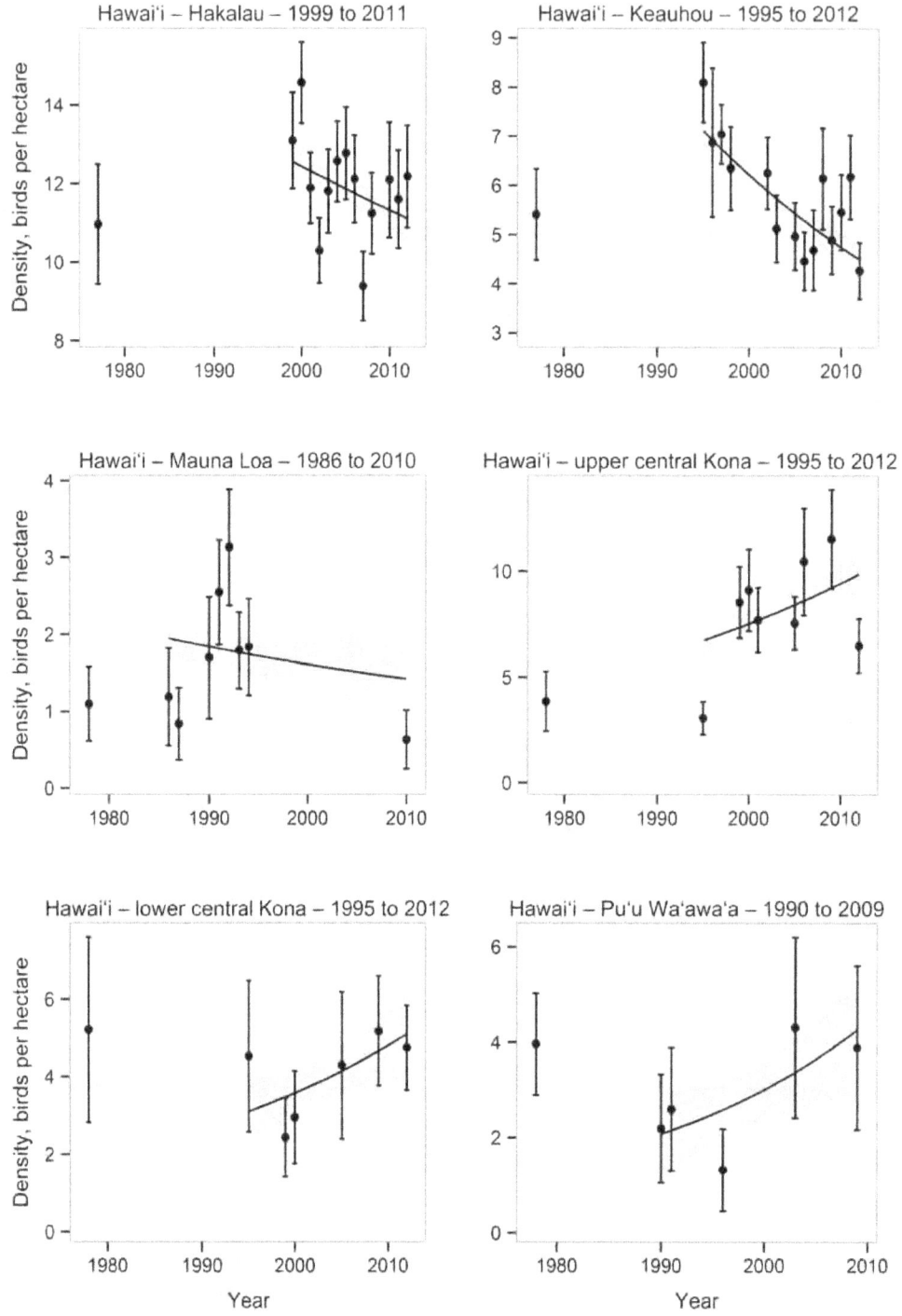

Figure 10. Trends in 'I'iwi (*Vestiaria coccinea*) density (mean birds per hectare at 95-percent confidence interval) in the Hakalau, Keauhou, Mauna Loa, the lower and upper portions of the central Kona, and the Pu'u Wa'awa'a consistently sampled areas (CSAs) of the island of Hawai'i, Hawai'i. The shaded band represents the 95-percentconfidence interval of the trend for the entire time series. Note that the 1977 and 1978 Hawai'i Forest Bird Survey densities were not included in the trend assessment because of differences in the time of year during which it and all subsequent surveys were conducted.

'I'iwi density within the Hakalau CSA of the north windward region appears to be stable-to-declining (fig. 10). That is, the slope for the 1999–2012 survey period ($\hat{\beta}$ = -0.0094 ± 0.0034; 95-percent CI = -0.0160 to -0.0027; table 2) showed strong evidence of a stable trend and weak evidence of a negative trend. This trend would result in an average 'I'iwi population decrease of 20 percent over a 25 year period. However, 'I'iwi showed no decreases in distribution at low elevations during 1977–2012 within the CSA (corresponding to the area sampled within the Hakalau Forest National Wildlife Refuge) (fig. 2). Although the CSA is situated above 1,400 m in elevation, and lies 3–4 km above the lower edge of the species range, 'I'iwi distribution in high-elevation forest has remained unchanged despite a possible slight decline in bird density.

Central Windward

The 'I'iwi species range in the central windward region includes a 40,773-ha area with an estimated 62,662–80,386 birds (mean = 71,524; table 1, appendix E.5), based on the densities observed in 2010 and 2012. A total of 98 percent of the estimated population occurs in montane mesic and wet forest, with few detections in montane dry-mesic grass-shrubland and none in other land cover types (appendix D.5). About 84 percent of the regional population is detected at elevations of 1,500–1,900 m, with the remainder observed at elevations ranging from as low as about 1,100 m to as high as 2,100 m.

'I'iwi densities show decreasing trends within the central windward region (table 2, fig. 10). A decline in 'I'iwi density is apparent for the Keauhou CSA, an area within the region in which the species is most abundant (3.7–4.8 birds per ha in 2012, mean = 4.3 ± 0.3 SE). The slope for the 1995–2012 survey period ($\hat{\beta}$ = -0.0270 ± 0.0033; 95-percent CI = -0.0334 to -0.0207; table 2) showed strong evidence of a negative trend, which would result in an average decline of 48 percent over a 25-year period. 'I'iwi in the Mauna Loa CSA show highly variable densities with a stable–to-downward trend ($\hat{\beta}$ = -0.0139 ± 0.0104; 95-percent CI = -0.0356–0.0051), and a projected decrease of 29 percent over 25 years.

The sparse set of observations available for the 'Ola'a CSA did not allow a quantitative assessment of the change in the elevational distribution of 'I'iwi. However, a qualitative appraisal of the number of birds per station (bps) indicates a fairly steady decline in bird occurrence: 1.0 bps in 1977, 0.4 bps in 1992, and 0.2 bps in 2010. The most current (2010) low-elevation record of 'I'iwi within the 'Ola'a CSA was at an elevation of 1,210 m, and 'I'iwi observed may have been visitors from higher elevations. These results may indicate that the species range in the region no longer extends into lowland wet forest (generally delimited by the 1,200-m elevation contour). Despite the declines in density apparent elsewhere in the central windward region, 'I'iwi occurrence did not show a pattern of elevation-range decreases within the Keauhou and Mauna Loa CSAs (fig. 11, appendixes F.5 and F.6). However, both of these areas lie almost entirely above 1,500 m in elevation, and consequently appear to be situated above the zone in which changes in distribution are evident.

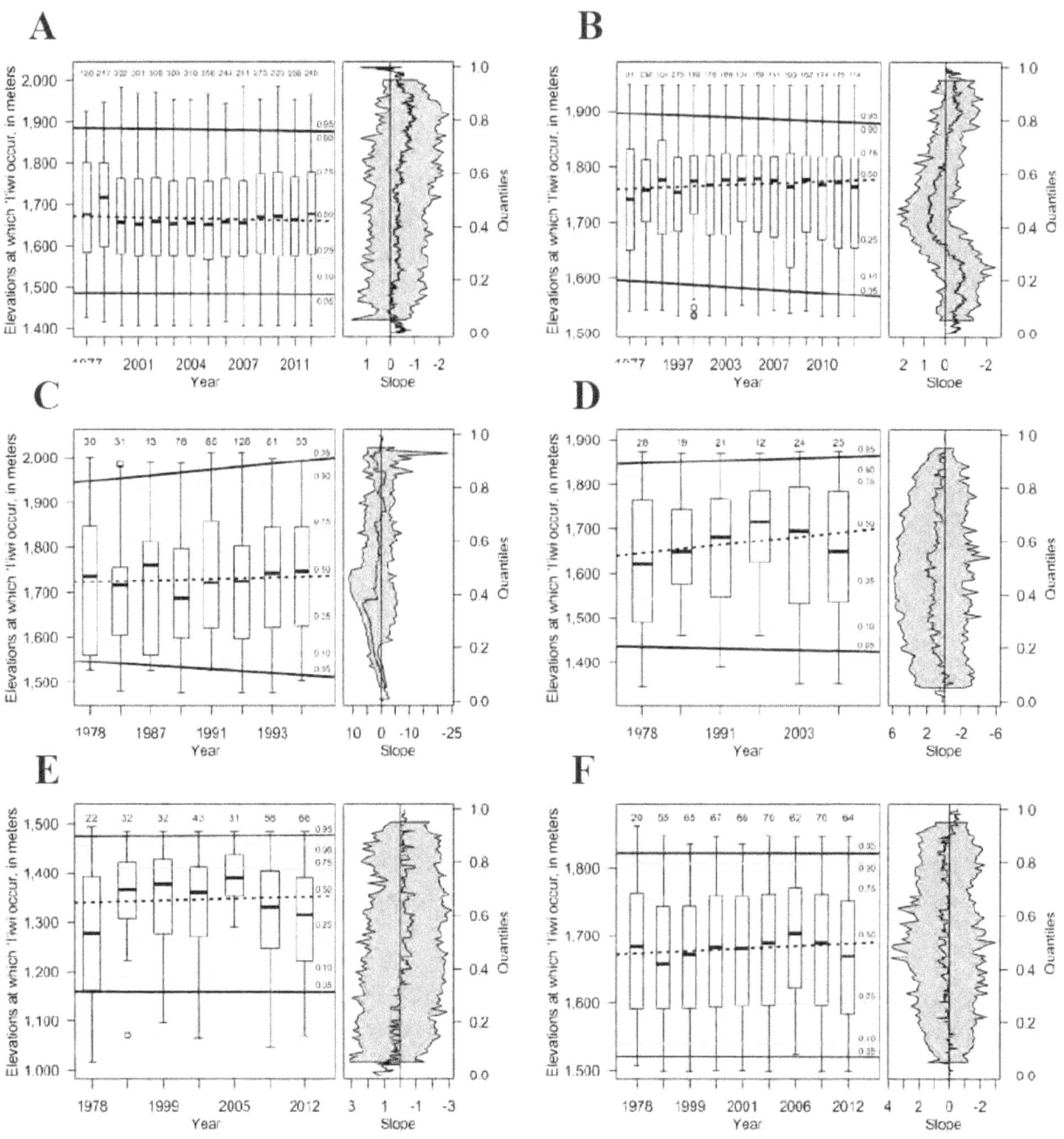

Figure 11. Trends in occurrence of ʻIʻiwi (*Vestiaria coccinea*) by elevation for island of Hawaiʻi consistently sampled areas (CSAs), Hawaiʻi. A) Hakalau CSA, with surveys from 1977, and 1999 to 2012; B) Keauhou CSA, with surveys from 1977, 1995, 1996, 1997, 1998, 2002, 2003, 2005, 2006, 2007, 2008, 2009, 2010, 2011, and 2012; C) Mauna Loa CSA, with surveys from 1978, 1986, 1987, 1990, 1991, 1992, 1993, and 1994; D) Puʻu Waʻawaʻa CSA, with surveys from 1978, 1990, 1991, 1996, 2003, and 2009; E) lower portion (elevations of 1,000–1,500 meters) central Kona CSA, with surveys from 1978, 1995, 1999, 2000, 2005, 2009, and 2012; and F) upper portion (elevations greater than 1,500 meters) central Kona CSA, with surveys from 1978, 1995, 1999, 2000, 2001, 2005, 2006, 2009, and 2012.

South Windward (Kaʻu)

The part of the ʻIʻiwi range that includes the Kaʻu region covers a 33,680-ha area with 23,138–33,512 birds (mean = 28,325; table 1, appendix E.6), based on the densities observed in 2004, 2008, and 2010. Most ʻIʻiwi are distributed in the northern half of the Kaʻu Forest Reserve (appendix D.6). About 94 percent of the population occurs in montane mesic and wet forest, with few recent (2004-2010) detections in lowland wet-mesic forest and none in other land cover types. Eighty-six percent of the regional population is about equally distributed from 1,300 to 1,900 m in elevation, with another 10 percent occurring as low as about 1,100 m, and the remaining few percent occurring as low as about 900 m and as high as 2,100 m (appendix E.6).

Despite the expected bias of underestimated densities associated with HFBS surveys, given they were surveyed in the summer when birds are widely distributed, the densities from recent (2004-2010) surveys are significantly lower for all three areas (north, central, and south) of Kaʻu (appendix G) compared to the HFBS surveys. At the forested north end of Kaʻu, the 1976 HFBS within the Kapapala Forest Reserve showed ʻIʻiwi to be about twice as abundant as they were in 2004 (2.7 [± 1.1 SE] versus 1.4 [± 1.1 SE] birds per ha)(Gorresen and others 2007). The 1976 HFBS within the central and main portion of the CSA also showed a three-fold decrease in density relative to that observed in 2008 (1.8 [± 0.1 SE] versus 0.6 [± 0.1 SE] birds per ha). Already uncommon during the 1978 HFBS (0.6 [± 0.2 SE] birds per ha), ʻIʻiwi were wholly absent from the south Kaʻu CSA in 2005 and 2010. Gorresen and others (2007) reported a total population of 78,154 birds at Kaʻu, based on 2002 surveys—a population estimate almost three times larger than the estimate in this report. Although ʻIʻiwi may have declined, more likely the discrepancies are owing to different count estimates from each survey creating large variations in density estimates, and, thus, in abundance estimates.

South Kona

The ʻIʻiwi range on the leeward side of the island of Hawaiʻi was divided into three regions to better reflect local differences in density and to improve population estimates: south Kona (12,489 ha), central Kona (25,441 ha), and north Kona (21,231 ha). The south Kona region has an estimated 2,059–4,918 birds (mean = 3,489; table 1), based on surveys conducted in 2003, 2009 and 2010. A total of 74 percent of the population occurs in montane mesic forest and 26 percent in montane wet forest, with no detections in other habitat types (appendix D.7 and E.7). About 21 percent of the regional population occurs within the 1,100–1,300-m elevation range, albeit at relatively low densities (0.3 [± 0.3 SE] birds per ha), with the remainder of ʻIʻiwi occurring as high as a little more than 1,700 m in elevation.

Assessments of density changes for the south Kona region only can be made in comparison to HFBS data. The south Kona area, with an elevation gradient of 960–1,640 m, showed a decrease in ʻIʻiwi density from 1978 (HFBS) to 2009 (2.6 [± 0.4 SE] versus 0.1 [± 0.1 SE] birds per ha; appendix G). The HFBS values are likely biased toward higher densities at low to mid elevations because of post-breeding dispersal, which suggests that the resulting decrease is likely greater than indicated. However, comparisons from the Honomalino area (appendix G) focus on the elevation gradient of 1,360–1,810 m, and indicates that density may have diminished from 2005 to 2010 (0.7 [± 0.2 SE] versus 0.4 [± 0.2 SE] birds per ha).

Central Kona

The central Kona region has an estimated ʻIʻiwi population of 124,649–155,009 birds (mean = 139,829; table 1) based on the densities observed in 2009 and 2010. About 96 percent of the population occurs in montane mesic and wet forest, with a small number of detections in lowland wet-mesic forest

25

and montane dry forest and woodland (appendix D.7). Ninety-two percent of the regional population occurs at elevations of 1,300–1,900 m. The 1,900–2,100m elevation range above the CSA has not been sampled since the 1978 HFBS, and 'I'iwi were not detected at that range during those surveys. However, this area may support about 420 birds (given the 4,300-ha area is composed mostly of montane dry forest and woodland, which has a mean density of 0.1 birds per ha elsewhere; appendix E.8).

'I'iwi density within the lower and upper portions of the CSA in the central Kona region appears to be increasing during the 1995–2012 survey period (fig. 10). The CSA spans an elevation gradient of 1,000–1,500 m (lower) and 1,500–1,900 m (upper). Slopes observed for both areas show strong evidence of positive trends (lower part: $\hat{\beta}$ = 0.0226 ± 0.0069; 95-percent CI = 0.0091–0.0361; upper part: $\hat{\beta}$ = 0.0294 ± 0.0130; 95-percent CI = 0.0043–0.0553; table 2). The average of these trends over a 25 year period would result in a 71 and a 97 percent increase in population size for lower and upper elevations, respectively.

The distribution of 'I'iwi (presence-absence) from 1978 to 2012 shows no decreases in 'I'iwi distribution at low elevations in the central Kona CSA (corresponding to most of the Kona Forest Unit of the Hakalau Forest National Wildlife Refuge; fig. 11). Bird distribution is annually variable in the lower portion of this area but shows no trend indicative of diminished occurrence in the 1,000–1,500 m or 1,500–1,900 m elevation ranges. However, habitat at elevations below the lower portion of the CSA (that is, less than 1,000 m) has not been surveyed since the 1978 HFBS, and a comparison to current survey results is not possible. Although relatively uncommon, 'I'iwi were detected at elevations as low as 400 m during the 1978 survey (that is, 47 detections at 65 stations, or about 0.7 birds per station, along HFBS transects 63, 64, and 65); however, this may indicate a post-breeding dispersal to low elevations. As elsewhere in leeward Hawai'i, it is unlikely that the current species range still includes habitat below elevations of 1,000 m in the central Kona region.

North Kona

The 'I'iwi population in north Kona seems restricted entirely to the northern and possibly the western slopes of Hualalai Volcano, and is estimated at 18,444–27,130 birds (mean = 22,787; table 1), based on survey results from 2003 and 2009. An extensive tract of degraded forest habitat lies between the populations in north Hualalai and central Kona, and much of this land cover likely is unsuitable habitat for resident 'I'iwi. 'I'iwi in the region were detected only in mesic forest, and at relatively moderate densities (3.7 [± 0.5 SE] birds per ha). About 1,135 ha of montane wet forest on west Hualalai was not sampled for birds, and may support 'I'iwi at a low density. Assuming a density one-half that of montane mesic forest (as observed in central Kona), montane wet forest in north Kona may contain about 2,043 additional birds. Lowland wet-mesic forest in the region lies entirely below elevations of 1,200 m, and given the infrequency of 'I'iwi detections at such elevations elsewhere in leeward Hawai'i, this habitat does not likely contribute substantially to the population estimate.

'I'iwi density within the Pu'u Wa'awa'a CSA in the north Kona region appears to have increased during the 1990–2009 survey period (fig. 10). The area spans an elevation range of 1,300–1,900 m (upper)(appendix D.7 and E.9). The regression slope shows strong evidence of a positive trend ($\hat{\beta}$ = 0.0383 ± 0.0163; 95-percent CI = 0.0075 to 0.0719; table 2), which is a 147-percent increase over 25 years. However, the time series for the CSA only is composed of 5 surveys over a 19-year period, and the 95-percent CI for the trend is relatively broad. Survey results from 1978 to 2009 demonstrate no decreases in 'I'iwi distribution at the lower elevations in the Pu'u Wa'awa'a CSA in the north Kona region (fig. 11).

Discussion

The status and trends of the 'I'iwi across the Hawaiian Islands for much of the last century have been characterized largely by low-elevation populations declining and higher-elevation populations remaining stable. 'I'iwi were described by early European visitors as one of the most common birds in all forests. If we use an estimate of 866,930 ha of potential forest habitat in pre-historical time (wet, mesic, and montane dry forests combined across all island; John Price, unpublished data) and the average density of 'I'iwi from high-elevation areas of Hakalau Forest National Wildlife Refuge (a place where 'I'iwi are one of the most common birds in the forest with 16.1 birds per ha), then there may have been as many as 13,870,896 'I'iwi just a few centuries ago. However, early descriptions of abundance were replaced by comments on 'I'iwi disappearing from low-elevation forests as early as the late 1800s (Banko, 1981). By the mid-1900s, 'I'iwi had virtually ceased to occur in low and mid-elevation forests, but high-elevation forests were still strongholds for the birds. In recent years, we see a continuation of that pattern. Populations on the lowest-elevation islands (specifically O'ahu, Lānai, and Moloka'i) have all but disappeared over the last hundred years, with possible remnant populations or rare visitors from neighboring high islands. Kaua'i, a mid-elevation island, has seen dramatic decreases in 'I'iwi populations over the last decade (2000-2012), with an estimated 96-percent decline over a 25-year period. However, even many of the high-elevation sites are showing signs of decline based on the most current surveys.

Estimating abundance and trends over a large and diverse area such as the entire Hawaiian archipelago was a difficult task. Although certain areas (continuously sampled areas [CSAs]) were surveyed multiple times over several decades, providing good information to evaluate trends, these CSAs represent a small part of the entire range of 'I'iwi, and typically at the higher elevations of the species' range. Similarly, abundance for the entire range, including many areas never surveyed, had to be extrapolated from a small part of the species' range in which surveys had been conducted. By stratifying density estimates into habitat types and elevational ranges, and extrapolating those densities by strata to unsurveyed areas, we were able to reasonably estimate 'I'iwi populations in unsurveyed areas. However, these are projections across areas with little or no information. Another difficulty, inherent in all time series of count data, is that each set of surveys is a random sample from the population across time, and these estimates will overcount or undercount the "true" population size by some unknown amount. Although distance analysis attempts to remove some of this variation, this variation results in density estimates that can fluctuate greatly from one survey to the next. Therefore, population estimates based on different surveys can result in large differences that may be owing in part to population trends, but also could be owing to simple sampling error.

'I'iwi are highly sensitive to disease, particularly avian malaria (Atkinson and others, 1995), and the prevalence of disease at low and middle elevations is believed to have largely determined the modern-day distribution of 'I'iwi. Avian malaria, transmitted by mosquitoes, is limited to low- and mid-elevation areas where the temperatures are sufficiently warm for the mosquitoes and the disease to develop (LaPointe and others, 2009). With global warming, rising temperatures are expected to facilitate the spread of mosquitoes and disease into high-elevation sanctuaries of the 'I'iwi (Benning and others, 2002), and unless the 'I'iwi develops resistance, such areas are not likely to support viable populations in the future. The trade wind cloud inversion layer (about 1,800–2,400 m elevation) caps precipitation at upper elevations and sets the effective tree line for the forest; the inversion zone is expected to persist into the future, potentially inhibiting forests from developing in higher-elevation areas (Cao and others, 2007). Therefore, the narrow elevation band in which 'I'iwi currently reside is expected to narrow further. 'I'iwi also are known to be highly mobile, flying across large areas to access flowering plants (Fancy and Ralph, 1998), and such movements can take them into areas where disease potentially is present (Kuntz, 2008). Therefore, the gradual retreat of 'I'iwi populations into increasingly higher elevation sanctuaries is likely owing to increasing temperatures, which increase the risk of disease, continued degradation of forest habitats, that also promote disease occurrence (LaPointe and others, 2009), amplified by high mobility of the 'I'iwi' and its sensitivity to disease.

Although disease is believed to be the main driver of the absence of 'I'iwi at low-to-mid elevations, other factors besides elevation interact with diseases and their vectors to influence the distribution of disease. For example, in the east region of Maui, 'I'iwi densities have increased, with detections as low as 860 m in elevation. This is well below typical elevations on the island of Hawai'i, where 'I'iwi rarely occur below 1,500 m, and even on Kaua'i, where 'I'iwi occur only above 1,000 m. The east region of Maui receives much annual precipitation (2–6 m), but surveys of the prevalence of mosquitoes and avian malaria detected very low prevalence rates in the Kīpahulu region of east Maui (Aruch and others, 2007). The study attributed low malaria rates in Kīpahulu to high rainfall events that flush larval mosquito habitats in stream drainages, and relatively cool temperatures even at low elevations that limit mosquito and malaria development. Additionally, the National Park Service has actively managed this area to control weeds and has eradicated feral pigs, removing the role that feral pigs have in creating standing water sources suitable for mosquito breeding (Atkinson and others, 1995). The forest habitats in the northeast and east regions of Maui also are large tracts of predominately native vegetation, without the ranching and urban-suburban development that degrade and fragment habitats introducing artificial water sources and corridors that allow mosquitoes to penetrate forests. Therefore, not only elevation, but quality of forest and sources of larval habitat seem critical in determining the distribution and abundance of 'I'iwi.

One interesting trend was the decrease in 'I'iwi at higher elevations in their range in some regions. This trend may be because of the degradation of upper-range habitat owing to continued persistent grazing by feral ungulates and drought conditions. Both forces have been shown to negatively affect bird populations (Banko and others, 2013). Another possibility is that as 'I'iwi populations decline, their distribution contracts inward to core habitat and away from marginal habitat. Most 'I'iwi occur in a narrow elevational band across the islands (Appendix E), with most trends suggesting this narrow band will get smaller. This highlights the importance of a relatively small area in which the 'I'iwi live—an area that is continuing to shrink.

Management and Research Considerations

1) **Rapidly assess distributional shifts:** Given concern about the status of 'I'iwi and evidence of population declines and distributional contractions across their range, we suggest establishing several transects that span the full elevational breadth of 'I'iwi occurrence on multiple islands as a long-term monitoring and early warning system for 'I'iwi (as well as for other birds of conservation concern). Ideally, such surveys would be conducted yearly, and would consist of a number of transects that strike a balance between a sufficient numbers to adequately describe general distributional trends, and yet not so many that the cost is prohibitive. Candidate locations for transects should use existing survey areas, and should be chosen for large elevational ranges, which may require establishing new stations at lower elevations to extend existing transects.

2) **Survey Kohala Mountains, Hawai'i:** The Kohala Mountains have not been surveyed since the late 1970s, at which time they supported an estimated 802 'I'iwi—a population much larger than any other remnant population at the time. Whether or not 'I'iwi exist there today is unknown, but if they persist in the Kohalas, they may represent an important disease-resistant population (see item 3). We suggest that a one-time survey of the Kohalas be undertaken to search for 'I'iwi, as well as other rare species.

3) Answer the question of whether isolated low-elevation 'I'iwi populations are important: West Maui, Moloka'i, Oahu, and possibly the Kohala Mountains represent low-elevation populations where disease is presumably present. These populations may be susceptible to disease and barely persisting, perhaps subsidized by high-elevation immigrants, or they may represent populations persisting in the presence of disease, and developing disease resistance. If these populations are persisting and are developing disease resistance, then they are very important populations for the long-term persistence of 'I'iwi. We suggest targeted research at one or more of these populations to 1) determine whether individuals present are resident and breeding, or are immigrants from neighboring high-elevation mountains; and 2) determine the prevalence of disease in the birds. If these populations are developing disease resistance, then efforts to protect the populations may be warranted to ensure that the evolution of disease resistance continues both to maintain the current low-elevation populations, and possibly to translocate to other areas where disease resistance has not evolved.

4) Understand drivers of Population declines: Populations decline when productivity or survival rates are insufficient to support stable populations, or emigration is high and immigration is low. Establishing demographic studies at several locations across the range of 'I'iwi would provide managers with the information on the actual drivers of population change (for example, reduced survival, reduced productivity). Although disease may be an important depressor of survival rates, productivity may be low, indicating problems beyond disease that may need to be managed. Ideally, several sites would be chosen to capture low-elevation dynamics (for example, at Kaua'i), as well as higher-elevation sites on Hawai'i and Maui.

5) Protect and expand high-elevation habitats: With evidence of 'I'iwi declining at low to medium elevations across much of its range, efforts to stabilize the species would best be directed at the core areas where populations are stable or increasing. Many of these core areas are protected or plans are underway to increase protection (such as fencing and ungulate exclusion), but efforts to increase habitat at higher elevations above these sites could help buffer populations to the effects of warming temperatures in the future.

Acknowledgments

This work is an analysis of over 30 years of intensive bird sampling by scores of people across some of the most difficult terrain and weather conditions observed anywhere in the world. We thank those dedicated surveyors for their hard work and dedication to the ecology and conservation of Hawai'i forest birds. Kevin Brinck made several important contributions to the analysis. Jack Jeffrey graciously provided the cover photo for this report. Funding was provided by the U.S. Fish and Wildlife Service Pacific Islands Office and the U.S. Geological Survey Pacific Island Ecosystems Research Center.

References Cited

Aruch, S., Atkinson, C.T., Savage, A.F., and LaPointe, D.A., 2007, Prevalence and distribution of pox-like lesions, avian malaria, and mosquito vectors in Kipahulu Valley, Haleakala National Park, Hawai'i, USA: Journal of Wildlife Diseases, v. 43, p. 567–575.

Atkinson, C.T., and LaPointe, D.A., 2009, Introduced avian diseases, climate change, and the future of Hawaiian Honeycreepers: Journal of Avian Medicine, v. 23, p. 53–63.

Atkinson, C.T., Woods, K.L., Dusek, R.J., Sileo, L.S., and Iko. W.M., 1995, Wildlife disease and conservation in Hawaii—Pathogenicity of avian malaria (*Plasmodium relictum*) in experimentally infected 'I'iwi (*Vestiaria coccinea*): Parasitology, v. 111, p. S59–S69.

Banko, P. C., and Banko, W.E., 2009, Evolution and ecology of food exploitation, chap. 7 *of* Pratt, T.K., Atkinson, C.T., Banko, P.C., Jacobi, J.D., and Woodworth, B.L., eds., Conservation biology of Hawaiian forest birds—Implications for island avifauna: New Haven, Connecticut, Yale University Press.

Banko, P.C., Camp, R.J., Farmer, C., Brinck, K.W., Leonard, D.L., and Stephens, R.M., 2013, Response of palila and other subalpine Hawaiian forest bird species to prolonged drought and habitat degradation by feral ungulates: Biological Conservation, v. 157, p. 70–77.

Banko, W.E., 1981, History of endemic Hawaiian birds, Part 1—Population histories—Species accounts, forest birds—*Vestiaria coccinea, Drepanis funereal, Drepanis pacifica*: Honolulu, Hawaii, University of Hawaii at Manoa, Cooperative National Park Resources Study Unit, Avian History Report 11 B.

Benning, T.L., LaPointe, D., Atkinson, C.T., and Vitousek, P.M., 2002, Interactions of climate change with biological invasions and land use in the Hawaiian Islands: Modeling the fate of endemic birds using a geographic information system; Proceedings of the National Academy of Sciences (USA), v. 99, p. 14246-14249.

BirdLife International. 2012. Species factsheet—*Vestiaria coccinea*: BirdLife International Web site, accessed May 6, 2012, at http://www.birdlife.org.

Buckland, S.T., Anderson, D.R., Burnham, K.P., and Laake, J.L., 2001, Distance sampling—Estimating abundance of biological populations: London, Chapman and Hall.

Buckland, S. T., Anderson, D.R., Burnham, K.P., Laake, J.L., Borchers, D.L., and Thomas, L., eds., 2004, Advanced distance sampling—Estimating abundance of biological populations, Oxford, United Kingdom, Oxford University Press.

Burnham, K.P., and Anderson, D.R., 2002, Model selection and multimodel inference: A practical information-theoretic approach. Springer, New York.

Cade, B.S., Terrell, J.W., and Schroeder, R.L,. 1999, Estimating effects of limiting factors with regression quantiles: Ecology, v. 80, p. 311–23.

Camp, R.J., Gorresen, P.M., Pratt, T.K., and Woodworth, B.L., 2009, Population trends of native Hawaiian forest birds, 1976–2008—The data and statistical analyses: Hawaii Cooperative Studies Unit Technical Report HCSU-012, 120 p.

Camp, R.J., Seavy, N.E., Gorresen, P.M., and Reynolds, M.H., 2008, A statistical test to show negligible trend—Comment: Ecology, v. 89, p. 1469–1472.

Cao, G., Giambelluca, T.W., Stevens, D.E., and Schroeder, T.A., 2007, Inversion variability in the Hawaiian trade wind regime: Journal of Climate, v. 20, p. 1145–1160.

Center for Biological Diversity, 2010, Petition to list the ʻIʻiwi (*Vestiaria coccinea*) as threatened or endangered under the U.S. Endangered Species Act: Center for Biological Diversity Web site, accessed December 1, 2012, at http://www.biologicaldiversity.org/ species/birds/iiwi/pdfs/Iiwi_Petition.pdf.

Conry, R., 1991, Oahu forest bird survey indicates decline in native species: Hawaii's Forests and Wildlife, v. 6, p. 2.

Fancy, S.G., and Ralph, C.J., 1998, ʻIʻiwi (*Vestiaria coccinea*), *in* Poole, A., and Gill, F., eds., The birds of North America, No. 327: Philadelphia, Birds of North America Inc.

Foster, J.T., Tweed, E.J., Camp, R.J., Woodworth, B.L., Adler, C.D., and Telfer, T., 2004, Long-term population changes of native and introduced birds in the Alaka'I Swamp, Kaua'I; Conservation Biology, v. 18, p. 716-725.

Gorresen, P.M., Camp, R.J., and Pratt, T.K., 2007, Forest bird distribution, density, and trends in the Ka`ū region of Hawai`i Island: U.S. Geological Survey Open-File Report 2007-1076, 101 p.

Hart, P.J., Woodworth, B.L., Camp, R.J., Turner, K., McClure, K., Goodall, K.,Henneman, C., Spiegel, C., Lebrun, J.,Tweed, E., and Samuel, M., 2011, Temporal variation in bird and resource abundance across an elevational gradient in Hawaii: Auk, v. 128, p. 113–126.

Hess, S.C., Banko, P.C., Reynolds, M.H., Brenner, G.J., Laniawe, L.P., and Jacobi, J.D., 2001, Drepanidine movements in relation to food availability in subalpine woodland on Mauna Kea, Hawai`i, in Scott, J.M., Conant, S., and Van Riper, C. III, eds., Evolution, ecology, conservation, and management of Hawaiian birds—A vanishing avifauna: Lawrence, Kansas, Allen Press, Cooper Ornithological Society, Studies in Avian Biology, no. 22, p. 154–163.

Kirch, P.V. 1982. The impact of the prehistoric Polynesians on the Hawaiian ecosystem. Pacific Science 36:1-14.

Koenker, R., 2007, Quantile regression in R—A vignette: The Comprehensive R Archive Network Web site, accessed 2/1/13, at *http://cran.r-project.org*.

Koenker, R., 2011, Quantreg—Quantile regression—R package version 4.62: The Comprehensive R Archive Network Web site, accessed 2/1/13, at:
http://crantastic.org/packages/quantreg/versions/11756.

Kuntz, W.A., 2008, The importance of individual behavior to life history and conservation—Breeding and movement biology in the I'iwi: Honolulu, University of Hawaii at Manoa, doctoral dissertation. 216 pp.

LaPointe, D.A., Atkinson, C.T., and Jarvi, S.I., 2009, Managing disease, chap. 17 *of* Pratt, T.K., Atkinson, C.T., Banko, P.C., Jacobi, J.D., and Woodworth, B.L., eds., Conservation biology of Hawaiian forest birds—Implication for island avifauna: New Haven, Connecticut, Yale University Press.

Lunn, D.J., Thomas, A., Best, N., and Spiegelhalter, D., 2000, WinBUGS—A Bayesian modelling framework—Concepts, structure, and extensibility: Statistics and Computing, v. 10, p. 325–337

Maindonald, J., and Braun, J., 2006. Data analysis and graphics using R—An example-based approach: Cambridge, United Kingdom, Cambridge University Press.

Munro, G.C. 1944. Birds of Hawai'i. Tongg Publishing, Honolulu.

National Audubon Society, 2002, The Christmas bird count historical results: National Audubon Web site, accessed May 6, 2013, at http://www.audubon.org/bird/cbc.

Nix, H.A. 1986, A biogeogaphic analysis of Australian Elapid snakes, *in* Longmore, R., ed., Atlas of Australian Elapid snakes: Australian Flora and Fauna Series 8, p. 4–15.

Paxton, E.H., Burgett, J., McDonald-Fadden, E., Bean, E., Atkinson, C.T., Ball, D., Cole, C., Crampton, L.H., Kraus, J., LaPointe, D.A., Mehrhoff, L., Samuel, M.D., Brewer, D.C., Converse, S.J., and Morey, S., 2012, Keeping Hawai'i's forest birds one step ahead of avian diseases in a warming world—A focus on Hakalau Forest National Wildlife Refuge: A case study from the National Conservation and Training Center Structured Decision Making Workshop, February 28–March 4, 2011, Hawai'i Volcanoes National Park, Hawaii.

Pratt, L.W., and Jacobi, J.D., 2009, Loss, degradation, and persistence of habitats, chap. 6 *of* Pratt, T.K., Atkinson, C.T., Banko, P.C., Jacobi, J.D., and Woodworth, B.L., eds., Conservation biology of Hawaiian forest birds—Implication for island avifauna: New Haven, Connecticut, Yale University Press.

Price, J.P., Jacobi, J.D., Pratt, L.W., Warchauer, F.R., and Smith, C.W., 2009, Protecting forest bird populations across landscapes, chap. 16 *of* Pratt, T.K., Atkinson, C.T., Banko, P.C., Jacobi, J.D., and Woodworth, B.L., eds., Conservation biology of Hawaiian forest birds—Implication for island avifauna: New Haven, Connecticut, Yale University Press.

R Development Core Team, 2011, R—A language and environment for statistical computing: Vienna, Austria, R Foundation for Statistical Computing.

Ralph, C.J., and Fancy, S.G., 1994, Timing of breeding and molting in six species of Hawaiian honeycreepers: Condor, v. 96, p. 151–161.

Scott, J.M., Mountainspring, S., Ramsey, F.L., and Kepler, C.B., 1986, Forest bird communities of the Hawaiian Islands—Their dynamics, ecology, and conservation: Lawrence, Kansas, Allen Press, Cooper Ornithological Society, Studies in Avian Biology, no. 9. 431 pp.

Scott, J.M., Ramsey, F.L., Lammertink, M., Rosenberg, K.V., Rohrbaugh, R., Wiens, J.A., and Reed. J.M., 2008, When is an "extinct" species really extinct?—Gauging the search efforts for Hawaiian forest birds and the Ivory-billed Woodpecker: Avian Conservation and Ecology–Écologie et conservation des oiseaux, v. 3, no. 2, article 3, accessed May 6, 2013, at http://www.ace-eco.org/vol3/iss2/art3/.

Shallenberger, R.J., and Vaughn, G.K., 1978, Avifaunal survey of the central Koolau Range, Oahu: Honolulu, Hawaii, Ahuimanu Productions, Honolulu.

Simon, J.C., Pratt, T.K., Berlin, K.E., Kowalsky, J.R., Fancy, S.G., and Hatfield, J.S., 2002, Temporal variation in bird counts within a Hawaiian rainforest: Condor, v. 104, p. 469–481.

Thomas, L., Buckland, S.T., Rexstad, E.A., Laake, J.L., Strindberg, S., Hedley, S.L., Bishop, J.R.B., Marques, T.A., and Burnham, K.P., 2010, Distance software: design and analysis of distance sampling surveys for estimating population size: Journal of Applied Ecology, v. 47, p. 5–14.

U.S. Fish and Wildlife Service, 1983, Kauai forest birds recovery plan: U.S. Fish and Wildlife Service, Portland, Oregon.

VanderWerf, E.A., and Rohrer, J.L., 1996, Discovery of an 'I'iwi population in the Koolau Mountains of Oahu: Elepaio, v. 56, p. 25–28.

Appendixes

Appendix A

Selection of 'I'iwi (*Vestiaria coccinea*) detection function models. Models were ranked by differences between each candidate model and the model with the lowest second-order Akaike's Information Criterion value (ΔAIC_c) after correcting for small sample size. Base models included half normal (H-norm) and hazard-rate (H-rate) key detection functions with cosine (Cos), hermite polynomial (H-poly) and simple polynomial (S-poly) adjustment terms. Covariates were incorporated with the highest AIC ranked base model. Covariates included survey region (Region; for the island of Hawai'i only), year of survey (Year), observer (Obs), detection type (Det; auditory [A], visual [V], both auditory and visual [B]), vegetation type (Veg), wind speed (Wind), gust speed (Gust), rain (Rain), and cloud cover (Cloud). For each model, the number of estimated parameters (Par), estimate of the log-likelihood (LogL) and AIC model weight (w_i) are provided. The top-ranked model for each island was used for estimation of bird density.

Island	Model	Adjustment terms	Covariates	Par	-LogL	AICc	ΔAICc	w_i
Kaua'i	H-rate	Key	Det	4	8,489.74	16,987.50	0.00	0.57
	H-rate	Key	[1]DetVB	3	8,491.04	16,988.09	0.59	0.43
	H-rate	Key	[2]DetAB	3	8,569.09	17,144.18	156.68	0.00
	H-rate	Key	Obs	32	8,546.19	17,157.45	169.95	0.00
	H-rate	Key	[3]Year	9	8,603.54	17,225.18	237.68	0.00
	H-rate	Key	Wind	5	8,625.00	17,260.04	272.54	0.00
	H-rate	Key	Cloud	5	8,632.18	17,274.39	286.89	0.00
	H-rate	[4]Key		2	8,636.20	17,276.42	288.92	0.00
	H-rate	[4]S-poly		3	8,635.86	17,277.74	290.24	0.00
	H-rate	[4]Cos		3	8,635.98	17,277.96	290.46	0.00
	H-rate	Key	Rain	4	8,635.71	17,279.45	291.95	0.00
	H-rate	Key	Veg	5	8,635.86	17,281.76	294.26	0.00
	H-rate	Key	Gust	5	8,638.92	17,287.86	300.36	0.00
	H-norm	[4]Cos		3	8,641.94	17,289.89	302.39	0.00
	H-rate	Key	[5]Year	3	8,642.15	17,290.30	302.80	0.00
	H-norm	[4]Key		1	8,661.68	17,325.37	337.87	0.00
	H-norm	[4]H-poly		2	8,661.30	17,326.61	339.11	0.00
Maui	H-rate	Key	Det	4	28,757.78	57,523.57	0.00	1.00
	H-rate	Key	[1]DetVB	3	28,777.46	57,560.91	37.34	0.00
	H-rate	Key	[2]DetAB	3	29,089.47	58,184.94	661.37	0.00
	H-rate	Key	Obs	29	29,244.67	58,547.58	1,024.01	0.00
	H-rate	Key	[3]Year	20	29,336.45	58,713.01	1,189.44	0.00
	H-rate	Key	Gust	7	29,435.78	58,885.57	1,362.00	0.00
	H-rate	Key	Veg	6	29,440.00	58,892.01	1,368.44	0.00
	H-rate	Key	[5]Year	3	29,447.45	58,900.89	1,377.32	0.00
	H-rate	Key	Wind	6	29,455.96	58,923.93	1,400.36	0.00
	H-rate	Key	Cloud	13	29,449.19	58,924.42	1,400.85	0.00
	H-rate	[4]Key		2	29,469.54	58,943.08	1,419.51	0.00
	H-rate	Key	Rain	6	29,465.55	58,943.12	1,419.55	0.00
	H-rate	[4]Cos		2	29,469.53	58,945.06	1,421.49	0.00

Island	Model	Adjustment terms	Covariates	Par	-LogL	AICc	ΔAICc	wᵢ
	H-norm	[4]H-poly		3	29,478.51	58,963.02	1,439.45	0.00
	H-norm	[4]Key		1	29,489.31	58,980.62	1,457.05	0.00
	[6]H-norm	[4]Cos		3	-	-	-	-
	[6]H-rate	[4]S-poly		3	-	-	-	-
Hawai'i	H-rate	Key	[1]DetVB	3	19,965.76	39,937.52	0.00	1.00
	H-rate	Key	Obs	14	20,165.88	40,359.85	422.33	0.00
	H-rate	Key	[2]DetAB	3	20,181.01	40,368.02	430.50	0.00
	H-rate	Key	[3]Year	6	20,296.70	40,605.41	667.89	0.00
	H-rate	Key	Veg	10	20,294.17	40,608.38	670.86	0.00
	H-rate	Key	Gust	4	20,314.78	40,637.56	700.04	0.00
	H-rate	Key	Cloud	13	20,307.37	40,640.82	703.30	0.00
	H-rate	Key	Wind	6	20,316.03	40,644.08	706.56	0.00
	H-rate	Cos		4	20,325.16	40,658.34	720.82	0.00
	H-norm	H-poly		3	20,326.20	40,658.34	720.88	0.00
	H-rate	[4]S-poly		2	20,327.92	40,659.84	722.32	0.00
	H-rate	Key		2	20,327.92	40,659.84	722.32	0.00
	H-rate	Key	[5]Year	3	20,327.50	40,661.00	723.48	0.00
	H-rate	Key	Rain	4	20,327.30	40,662.61	725.09	0.00
	H-rate	Key	Elev	3	20,328.86	40,663.72	726.20	0.00
	H-norm	[4]Cos		1	20,337.86	40,677.71	740.19	0.00
	H-norm	Key		1	20,337.86	40,677.71	740.19	0.00
	[6]H-rate	Key	Det	4	-	-	-	-

[1] Detection types V and B pooled

[2] Detection types A and B pooled

[3] Year treated as a categorical variable (that is, factor)

[4] Base model

[5] Year treated as a continuous variable

[6] Model failed to converge

Appendix B

Effective detection radius (EDR) from top-ranked 'I'iwi (*Vestiaria coccinea*) detection function model by island. EDR mean, standard error (SE), and 95-percent (95%) confidence interval (CI) are presented separately for each model covariate.

Island	Model	Covariate	Covariate EDR (mean ± SE)	Covariate EDR (95% CI)
Kaua'i	H-rate Key	auditory	49.918 ± 1.017	47.962-51.953
		auditory and visual	22.315 ± 1.060	20.326-24.499
Maui	H-rate Key	auditory	40.739 ± 0.327	40.103-41.385
		visual	16.239 ± 0.503	15.282-17.256
		auditory and visual	22.725 ± 0.489	21.785-23.706
Hawai'i	H-rate Key	auditory	45.151 ± 0.515	44.153-46.172
		auditory and visual	24.327 ± 0.505	23.355-25.338

Appendix C

Landfire2 land cover types reclassified to consolidate categories and to derive a sufficient number of survey observations for developing 'I'iwi (*Vestiaria coccinea*) detection models.

Original land cover class	Revised class
Hawai'i lowland dry forest	Lowland dry forest
Hawai'i lowland dry grassland	Lowland dry-mesic grassland-shrubland
Hawai'i lowland dry shrubland	Lowland dry-mesic grassland-shrubland
Hawai'i lowland mesic forest	Lowland wet-mesic forest
Hawai'i lowland mesic grassland	Lowland dry-mesic grassland-shrubland
Hawai'i lowland mesic shrubland	Lowland dry-mesic grassland-shrubland
Hawai'i lowland rainforest	Lowland wet-mesic forest
Hawai'i montane rainforest	Montane wet forest
Hawai'i montane-subalpine dry forest and woodland	Montane dry forest and woodland
Hawai'i montane-subalpine dry grassland	Montane dry-mesic grass-shrubland
Hawai'i montane-subalpine dry shrubland	Montane dry-mesic grass-shrubland
Hawai'i montane-subalpine mesic forest	Montane mesic forest
Hawai'i montane-subalpine mesic grassland	Montane dry-mesic grass-shrubland
Hawaiian introduced deciduous shrubland	Introduced grass-shrubland
Hawaiian introduced dry forest	Introduced forest
Hawaiian introduced evergreen shrubland	Introduced grass-shrubland
Hawaiian introduced perennial grassland	Introduced grass-shrubland
Hawaiian introduced wet-mesic forest	Introduced forest
Hawaiian managed tree plantation	Introduced forest
Barren	Barren
Agriculture-cultivated crops and irrigated agriculture	Other
Developed-low intensity	Other
Developed-medium intensity	Other
Developed-high intensity	Other
Developed-open space	Other

Appendix D

Location and abundance of 'I'iwi based on the most recent surveys (see figure captions for year).

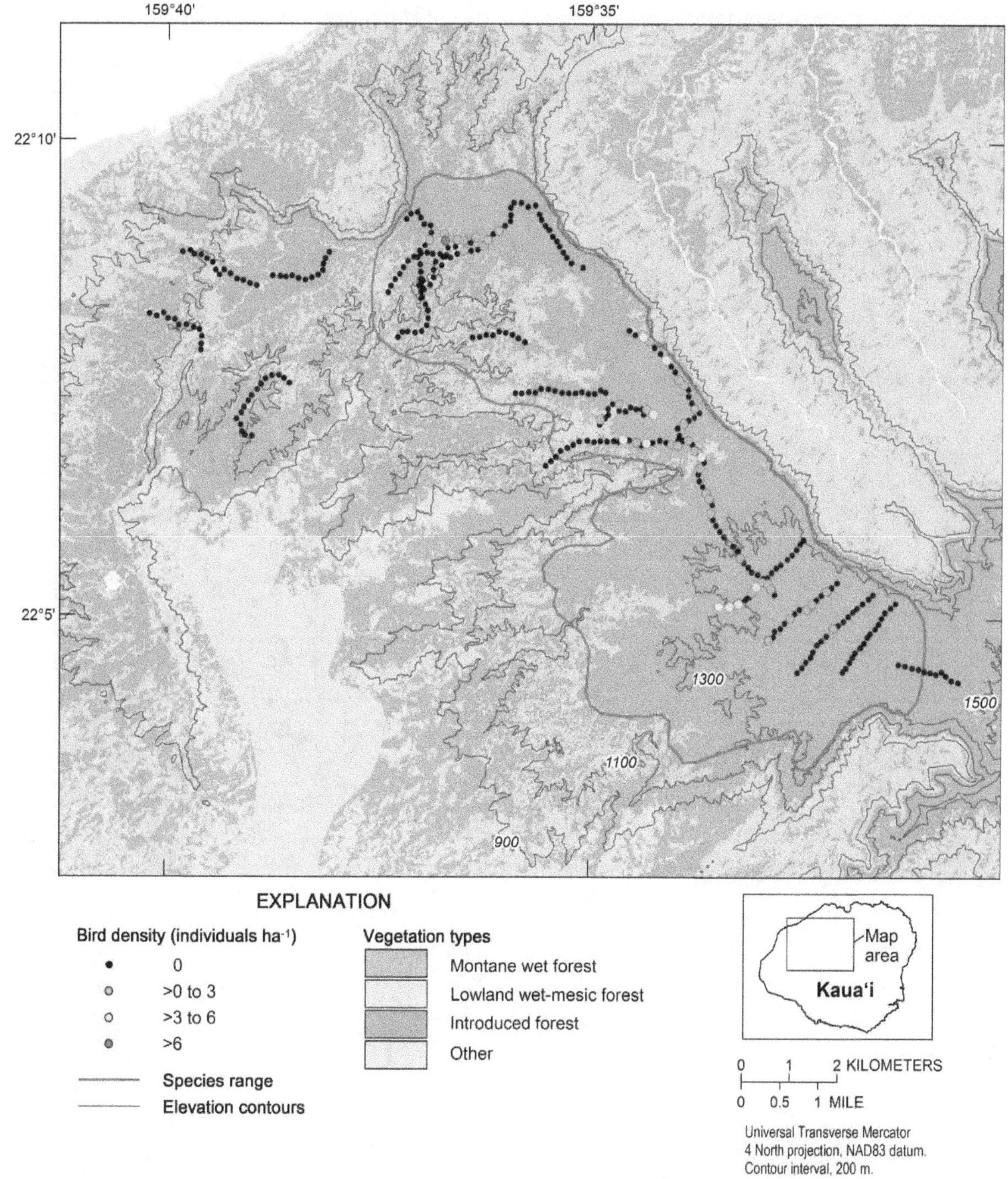

EXPLANATION

Bird density (individuals ha⁻¹)

●	0
○	>0 to 3
○	>3 to 6
●	>6

‒‒‒‒‒ Species range

‒‒‒‒‒ Elevation contours

Vegetation types

- Montane wet forest
- Lowland wet-mesic forest
- Introduced forest
- Other

Kaua'i — Map area

0   1   2 KILOMETERS
0   0.5   1 MILE

Universal Transverse Mercator
4 North projection, NAD83 datum.
Contour interval, 200 m.

D.1: 'I'iwi (*Vestiaria coccinea*) distribution and abundance on Kaua'i, Hawai'i. The vegetation types and elevation contours shown correspond to strata for which density and abundance were estimated for the area within the species range (red outline; appendix E.1). Density per station values (points) are derived from survey counts conducted in 2012.

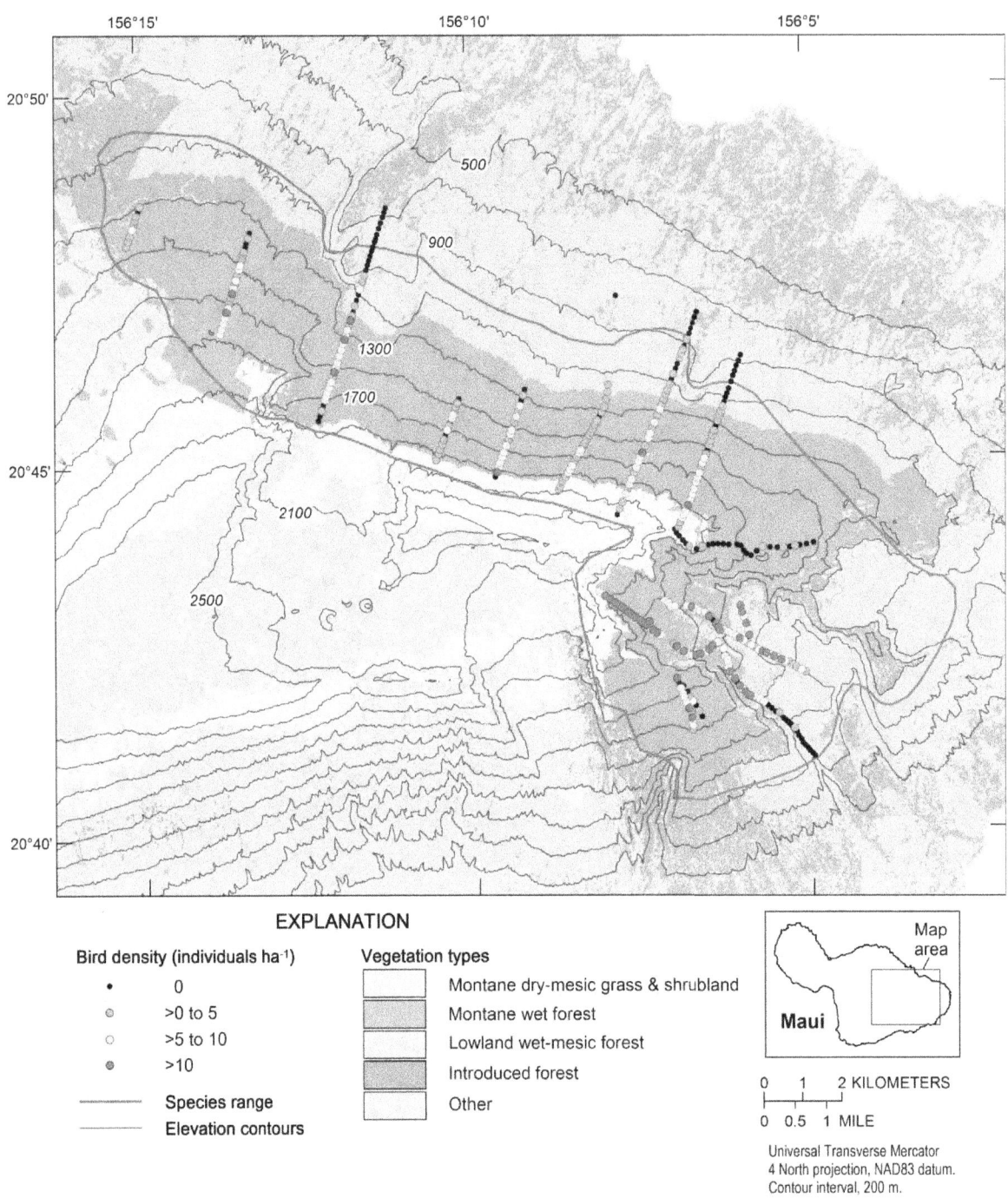

EXPLANATION

Bird density (individuals ha⁻¹)

- •   0
- ◎   >0 to 5
- ○   >5 to 10
- ◉   >10

     Species range

     Elevation contours

Vegetation types

     Montane dry-mesic grass & shrubland

     Montane wet forest

     Lowland wet-mesic forest

     Introduced forest

     Other

Map area

Maui

0   1   2 KILOMETERS

0   0.5   1 MILE

Universal Transverse Mercator
4 North projection, NAD83 datum.
Contour interval, 200 m.

D.2: ʻIʻiwi (*Vestiaria coccinea*) distribution and abundance on east Maui, Hawaiʻi. The vegetation types and elevation contours shown correspond to strata for which density and abundance were estimated for the area within the species range (red outline; appendix E.2). Density per station values (points) are derived from survey counts made in 2011 and 2012.

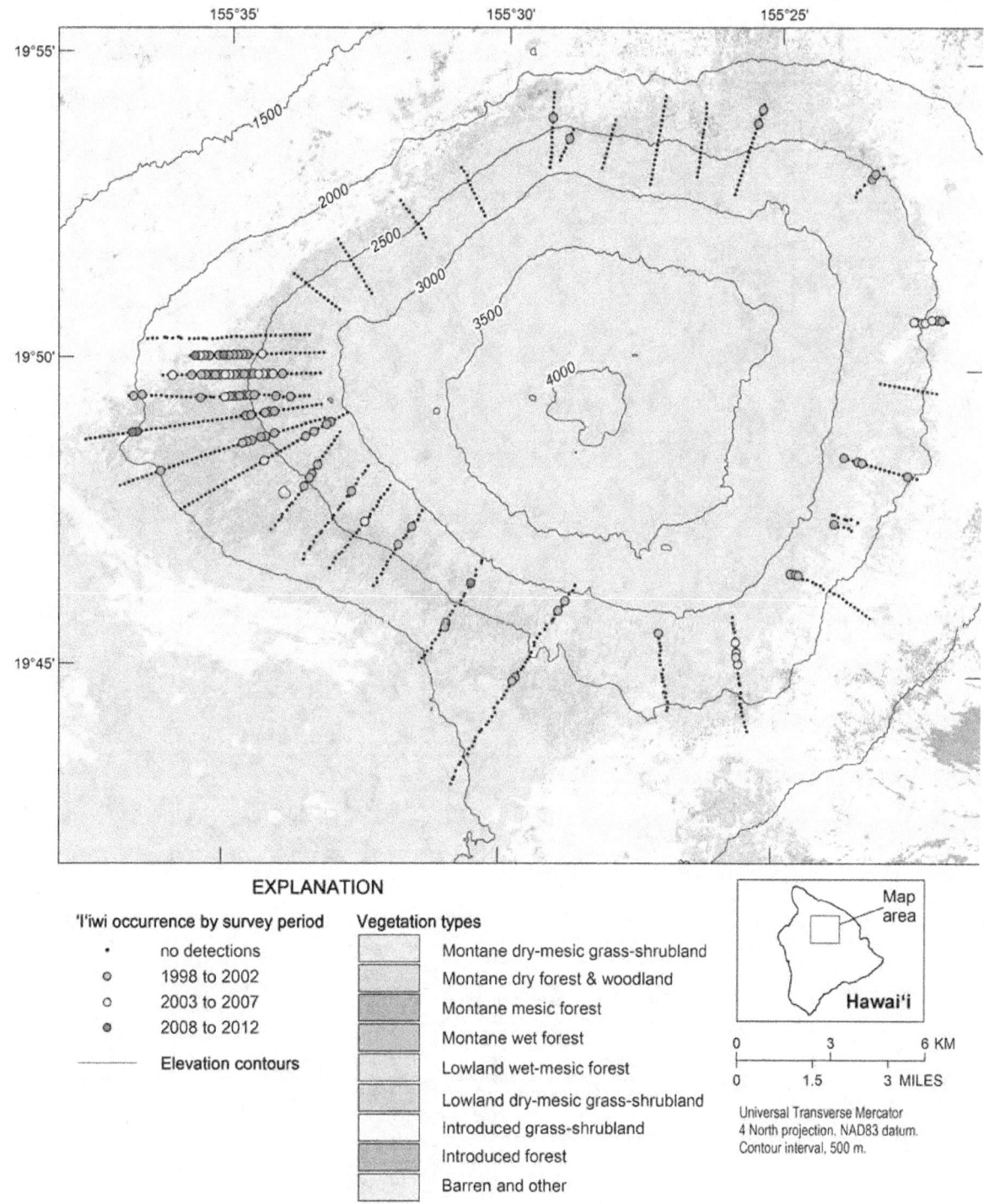

D.3: 'I'iwi (*Vestiaria coccinea*) distribution in the Mauna Kea region of the island of Hawai'i, Hawai'i. Occurrence records (points) are grouped by a 5-year interval for surveys made between 1998 and 2012.

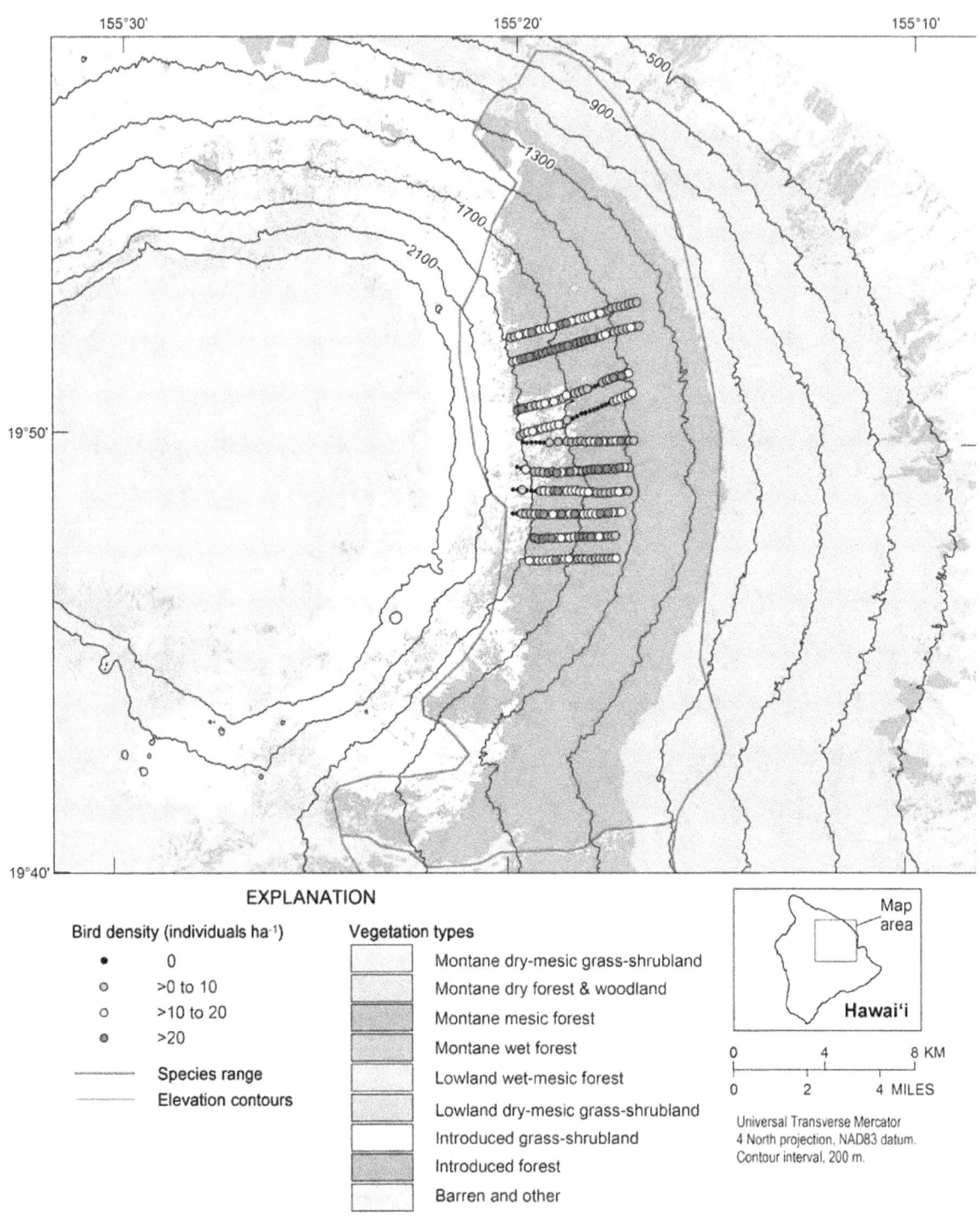

D.4: 'I'iwi (*Vestiaria coccinea)* distribution and abundance in the north windward region of the island of Hawai'i, Hawai'i. The vegetation types and elevation contours shown correspond to strata for which density and abundance were estimated for the area within the species range (red outline; appendix E.4). Density per station values (points) are derived from survey counts made in 2012.

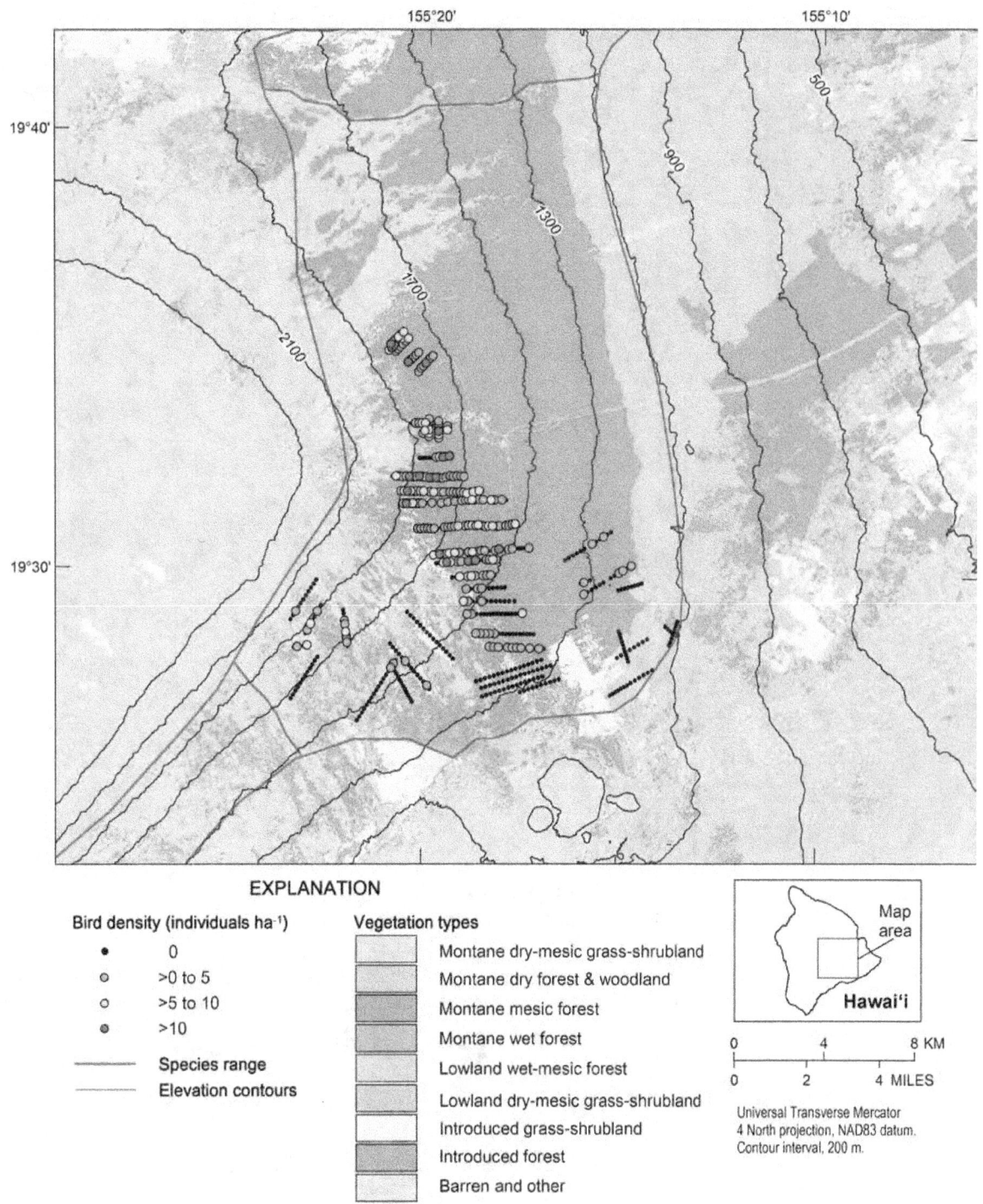

EXPLANATION

Bird density (individuals ha⁻¹)

- ● 0
- ◎ >0 to 5
- ○ >5 to 10
- ◉ >10

—— Species range

—— Elevation contours

Vegetation types

Montane dry-mesic grass-shrubland
Montane dry forest & woodland
Montane mesic forest
Montane wet forest
Lowland wet-mesic forest
Lowland dry-mesic grass-shrubland
Introduced grass-shrubland
Introduced forest
Barren and other

Map area

Hawai'i

0   4   8 KM
0   2   4 MILES

Universal Transverse Mercator
4 North projection, NAD83 datum.
Contour interval, 200 m.

D.5: 'I'iwi (*Vestiaria coccinea)* distribution and abundance in the central windward region of the island of Hawai'i, Hawai'i. The vegetation types and elevation contours shown correspond to strata for which density and abundance were estimated for the area within the species range (red outline; appendix E.5). Density per station values (points) are derived from survey counts made in 2010 and 2012.

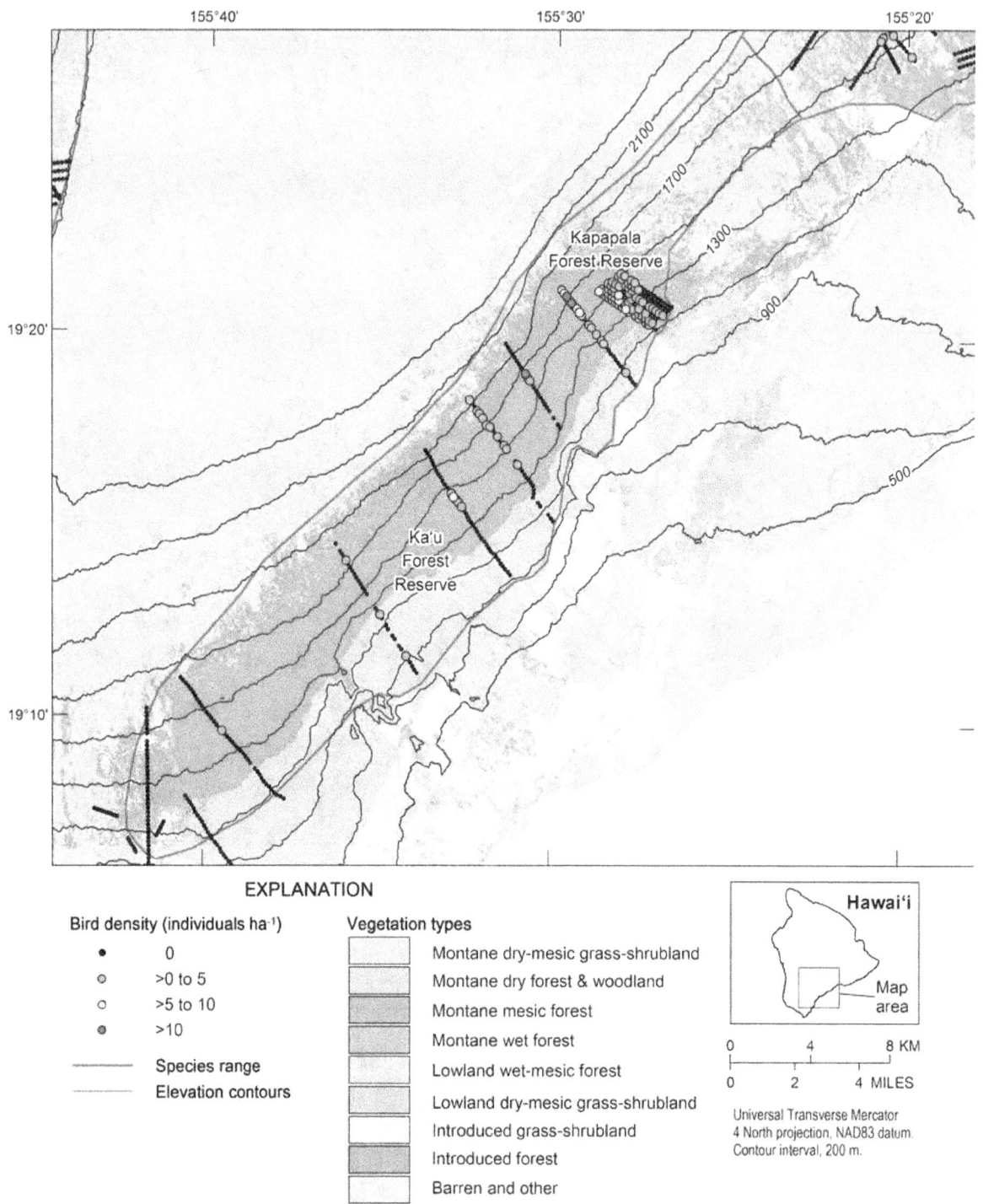

D.6: 'I'iwi (*Vestiaria coccinea*) distribution and abundance in the Ka'u region of the island of Hawai'i. The vegetation types and elevation contours shown correspond to strata for which density and abundance were estimated for the area within the species range (red outline; appendix E.6). Density per station values (points) are derived from survey counts made in 2004, 2008, and 2010.

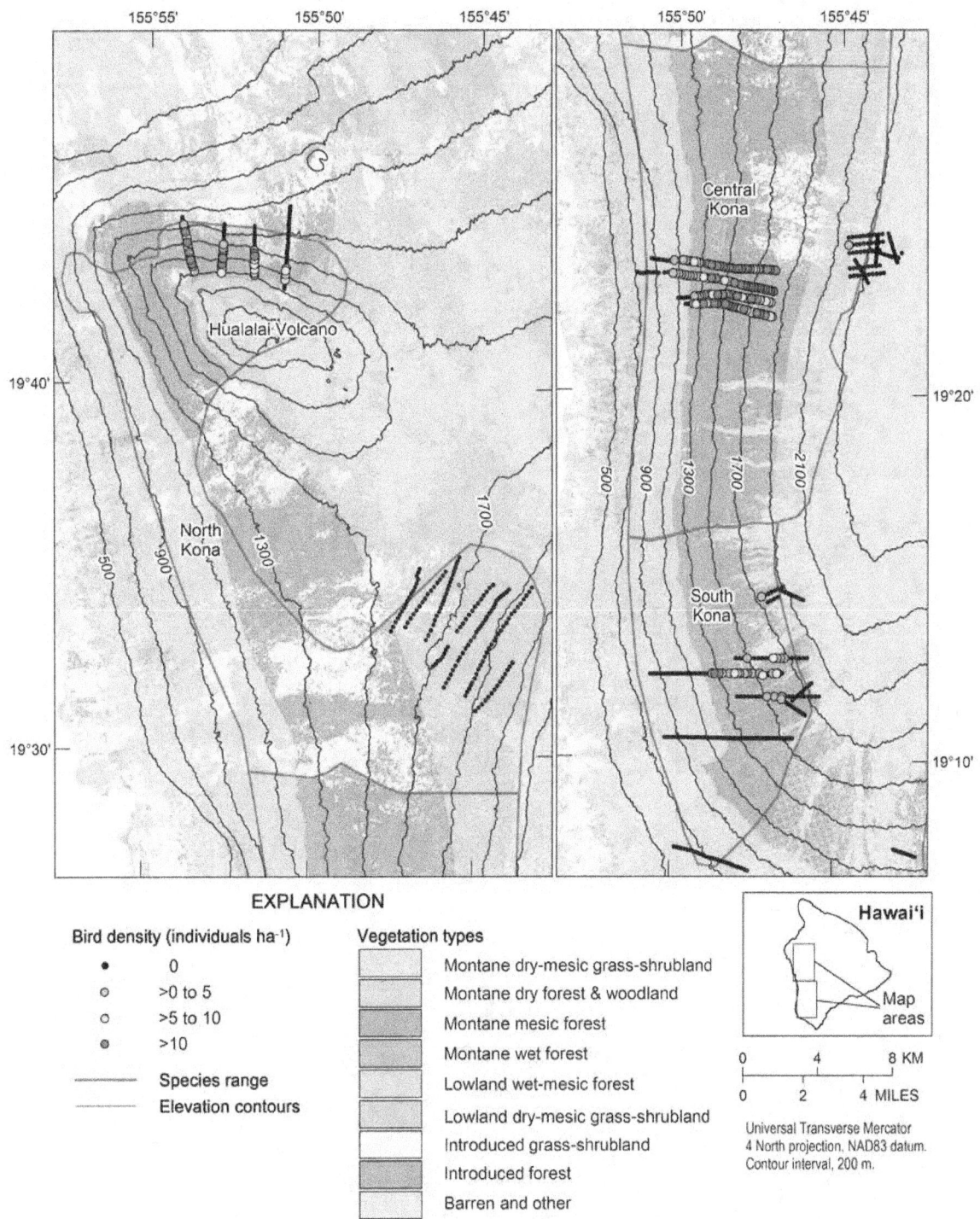

Bird density (individuals ha⁻¹)

- •   0
- ○   >0 to 5
- ○   >5 to 10
- ◉   >10

——— Species range

········· Elevation contours

Vegetation types

- Montane dry-mesic grass-shrubland
- Montane dry forest & woodland
- Montane mesic forest
- Montane wet forest
- Lowland wet-mesic forest
- Lowland dry-mesic grass-shrubland
- Introduced grass-shrubland
- Introduced forest
- Barren and other

0   4   8 KM

0   2   4 MILES

Universal Transverse Mercator
4 North projection, NAD83 datum.
Contour interval, 200 m.

D.7: 'I'iwi distribution and abundance in the Kona region of the island of Hawai'i, Hawai'i (depicted separately for the north Kona region [left panel] and the central and south Kona regions [right panel]). The vegetation types and elevation contours shown correspond to strata for which density and abundance were estimated for the area within the species range (red outline; appendixes E.7, E.8., and E.9). Density per station values (points) are derived from survey counts made in 2003 and 2009 (north Kona), 2009 and 2010 (central Kona), and 2003, 2009, and 2010 (south Kona).

Appendix E

Density and population abundance estimates by elevation and vegetation type for the area encompassed by the species range. Year of survey from which estimates are derived is specified following each island- or region-specific name. Sample size (number of stations sampled) and detections (number of birds observed) are indicated with *K* and *n*, respectively. Total population density (birds per hectare) and abundance by habitat variable for all strata are summarized in shaded rows. Unsampled strata do not contribute to population abundance estimates, but are included to provide areas used in the species range size values specific to islands or island-regions.

E.1: Kaua'i – survey year 2012

Habitat variable	Stratum	Area (ha)	K	n	Mean density	SE	CV (%)	Lower 95% CI	Upper 95% CI	Mean abundance	SE	CV (%)	Lower 95% CI	Upper 95% CI
Elevation	900-1,100 m	266	19	1	0.093	0.102	110	0.000	0.333	25	27	110	0	89
	1,100-1,300 m	3,808	172	54	0.563	0.110	20	0.370	0.789	2,143	419	20	1,411	3,004
	1,300-1,500 m	1,385	76	15	0.314	0.089	28	0.160	0.499	435	124	28	222	691
	all sampled strata	5,459	267	70	0.477	0.083	17	0.328	0.645	2,603	453	17	1,789	3,520
Vegetation	Montane wet forest	4,587	216	61	0.486	0.090	18	0.324	0.675	2,227	412	18	1,482	3,091
	Lowland wet-mesic forest	825	51	9	0.340	0.133	39	0.105	0.611	271	106	39	84	487
	Introduced forest	47	0	-	-	-	-	-	-	-	-	-	-	-
	all sampled strata	¹5,412	267	70	0.464	0.081	18	0.319	0.640	2,498	437	18	1,718	3,442

E.2: East Maui – survey years 2011 and 2012

Habitat variable	Stratum	Area (ha)	K	n	Mean density	SE	CV (%)	Lower 95% CI	Upper 95% CI	Mean abundance	SE	CV (%)	Lower 95% CI	Upper 95% CI
Elevation	500-700 m	83	0	-	-	-	-	-	-	-	-	-	-	-
	700-900 m	824	22	4	0.557	0.321	58	0.000	1.254	459	264	58	0	1,033
	900-1,100 m	1,979	30	50	3.465	0.937	27	1.955	5.568	6,859	1,855	27	3,870	11,021
	1,100-1,300 m	2,817	52	128	4.613	0.676	15	3.361	6.035	12,996	1,904	15	9,470	17,001
	1,300-1,500 m	2,555	68	188	3.990	0.466	12	3.115	4.969	10,193	1,191	12	7,958	12,696
	1,500-1,700 m	2,249	87	344	5.865	0.453	8	5.039	6.737	13,189	1,020	8	11,331	15,149
	1,700-1,900 m	1,576	53	364	6.873	0.572	8	5.798	8.117	10,829	901	8	9,136	12,614
	1,900-2,100 m	1,035	28	183	4.597	0.644	14	3.345	5.970	4,760	667	14	3,463	6,181
	2,100-2,300 m	358	2	2	0.345	0.241	70	0.000	0.734	123	86	70	0	262
	2,300-2,500 m	8	0	-	-	-	-	-	-	-	-	-	-	-
	all sampled strata	¹13,393	342	1,263	4.436	0.292	7	3.873	5.019	59,407	3,915	7	51,874	67,218
Vegetation	Montane dry-mesic grass-shrubland	907	24	128	3.517	0.719	20	2.117	4.919	3,189	652	20	1,919	4,461
	Montane wet forest	7,812	237	1,015	5.648	0.345	6	4.986	6.314	44,124	2,696	6	28,949	49,320
	Lowland wet-mesic forest	3,495	77	117	3.174	0.502	16	2.286	4.347	11,092	1,756	16	7,989	15,194
	Introduced forest	794	4	3	2.399	1.300	54	0.000	4.983	1,906	1,033	54	0	3,959
	all sampled strata	13,008	342	1,263	4.636	0.286	6	4.102	5.179	60,310	3,715	6	53,356	67,363

45

E.3: Hawai'i (all regions)

Habitat variable	Stratum	Area (ha)	K	n	Mean density	SE	CV (%)	Lower 95% CI	Upper 95% CI	Mean abundance	SE	CV (%)	Lower 95% CI	Upper 95% CI
Elevation	all sampled strata	[1]174,579	1,852	2,798	3.465	0.119	3	3.242	3.699	531,868	18,198	3	497,655	567,911
Vegetation	all sampled strata	[1]175,100			3.417	0.125	4	3.174	3.654	554,150	20,272	4	514,708	592,558

E.4: Hawai'i, north windward – survey year 2012

Habitat variable	Stratum	Area (ha)	K	n	Mean density	SE	CV (%)	Lower 95% CI	Upper 95% CI	Mean abundance	SE	CV (%)	Lower 95% CI	Upper 95% CI
Elevation	700-900 m	474	0	-	-	-	-	-	-	-	-	-	-	-
	900-1,100 m	2,046	0	-	-	-	-	-	-	-	-	-	-	-
	1,100-1,300 m	6,807	0	-	-	-	-	-	-	-	-	-	-	-
	1,300-1,500 m	8,599	19	86	7.807	0.659	8	6.556	9.031	67,135	5,670	8	56,373	77,660
	1,500-1,700 m	7,608	125	684	13.279	1.034	8	11.390	15.289	101,025	7,870	8	86,652	116,322
	1,700-1,900 m	4,887	105	634	16.113	1.149	7	13.932	18.377	78,744	5,616	7	68,087	89,807
	1,900-2,100 m	1,784	16	27	5.021	2.337	47	1.158	9.934	8,957	4,169	47	2,066	17,722
	2,100-2,300 m	350	0	-	-	-	-	-	-	-	-	-	-	-
	all sampled strata	[1]22,878	265	1,431	11.184	0.533	5	10.142	12.213	255,861	12,205	5	232,023	279,406
Vegetation	Montane dry-mesic grass-shrubland	255	0	-	-	-	-	-	-	-	-	-	-	-
	Montane dry forest & woodland	1	0	-	-	-	-	-	-	-	-	-	-	-
	Montane mesic forest	4,701	103	509	11.579	1.155	10	9.318	13.894	54,432	5,428	10	43,804	65,314
	Montane wet forest	18,198	162	922	13.398	0.779	6	11.909	14.985	243,816	14,183	6	216,723	272,705
	Lowland wet-mesic forest	4,904	0	-	-	-	-	-	-	-	-	-	-	-
	Lowland dry-mesic grass-shrubland	45	0	-	-	-	-	-	-	-	-	-	-	-
	Introduced grass-shrubland	4,075	5	0	0	0	0	0	0	0	0	0	0	0
	Introduced forest	324	0	-	-	-	-	-	-	-	-	-	-	-
	Barren and other	161	0	-	-	-	-	-	-	-	-	-	-	-
	all sampled strata	[1]26,974	270	1,431	11.057	0.558	5	10.024	12.172	298,249	15,038	5	270,393	328,335

E.5: Hawai'i, central windward – survey years 2010 and 2012

Habitat variable	Stratum	Area (ha)	K	n	Mean density	SE	CV (%)	Lower 95% CI	Upper 95% CI	Mean abundance	SE	CV (%)	Lower 95% CI	Upper 95% CI
Elevation	900-1,100 m	78	0	-	-	-	-	-	-	-	-	-	-	-
	1,100-1,300 m	10,030	76	10	0.205	0.098	48	0.041	0.411	2,061	979	48	412	4,121
	1,300-1,500 m	9,946	153	34	0.316	0.077	24	0.183	0.480	3,141	763	24	1,819	4,773
	1,500-1,700 m	9,117	140	187	2.854	0.305	11	2.274	3.441	26,020	2,781	11	20,732	31,371
	1,700-1,900 m	7,668	153	303	4.207	0.372	9	3.547	4.997	32,259	2,852	9	27,197	38,317
	1,900-2,100 m	3,739	19	18	1.680	0.676	40	0.493	3.142	6,282	2,527	40	1,844	11,747
	2,100-2,300 m	358	0	-	-	-	-	-	-	-	-	-	-	-
	all sampled strata	40,500	541	552	1.723	0.121	7	1.502	1.970	69,763	4,912	7	60,838	79,772
Vegetation	Montane dry-mesic grass-shrubland	6,089	41	2	0.245	0.170	69	0	0.622	1,494	1,037	69	0	3,788
	Montane dry forest & woodland	491	2	0	0	0	0	0	0	0	0	0	0	0
	Montane mesic forest	8,009	304	380	2.376	0.193	8	2.009	2.761	19,026	1,546	8	16,088	22,116
	Montane wet forest	16,643	106	170	3.170	0.441	14	2.365	4.074	52,765	7,335	14	39,362	67,802
	Lowland wet-mesic forest	4,295	38	0	0	0	0	0	0	0	0	0	0	0
	Lowland dry-mesic grass-shrubland	32	0	-	-	-	-	-	-	-	-	-	-	-
	Introduced grass-shrubland	1,402	32	0	0	0	0	0	0	0	0	0	0	0
	Introduced forest	150	3	0	0	0	0	0	0	0	0	0	0	0
	Barren and other	3,966	15	0	0	0	0	0	0	0	0	0	0	0
	all sampled strata	41,045	541	552	1.785	0.185	10	1.447	2.180	73,285	7,592	10	59,393	89,483

E.6: Hawai'i, Ka'ū – survey years 2004, 2008, and 2010

Habitat variable	Stratum	Area (ha)	K	n	Mean density	SE	CV (%)	Lower 95% CI	Upper 95% CI	Mean abundance	SE	CV (%)	Lower 95% CI	Upper 95% CI
Elevation	700-900 m	682	5	0	0	0	0	0	0	0	0	0	0	0
	900-1,100 m	3,883	31	2	0.101	0.069	69	0	0.252	391	268	69	0	978
	1,100-1,300 m	6,461	130	44	0.528	0.115	22	0.312	0.769	3,414	742	22	2,018	4,970
	1,300-1,500 m	6,302	116	87	1.270	0.189	15	0.920	1.660	8,002	1,189	15	5,797	10,462
	1,500-1,700 m	7,184	67	55	1.738	0.374	22	1.113	2.523	12,482	2,690	22	7,999	18,124
	1,700-1,900 m	5,932	22	13	1.443	0.607	42	0.426	2.808	8,561	3,602	42	2,526	16,654
	1,900-2,100 m	3,299	7	1	0.223	0.198	89	0	0.669	736	652	89	0	2,208
	2,100-2,300 m	151	0	-	-	-	-	-	-	-	-	-	-	-
	all sampled strata	¹33,743	378	202	0.995	0.137	14	0.748	1.290	33,587	4,624	14	25,242	43,531
Vegetation	Montane dry-mesic grass-shrubland	5,070	3	0	0	0	0	0	0	0	0	0	0	0
	Montane dry forest & woodland	353	0	-	-	-	-	-	-	-	-	-	-	-
	Montane mesic forest	7,513	163	130	1.422	0.203	14	1.047	1.846	10,684	1,527	14	7,868	13,866
	Montane wet forest	13,127	131	64	0.838	0.149	18	0.564	1.158	11,005	1,957	18	7,403	15,195
	Lowland wet-mesic forest	7,045	64	8	0.195	0.091	47	0.024	0.390	1,375	642	47	172	2,750
	Lowland dry-mesic grass-shrubland	45	0	-	-	-	-	-	-	-	-	-	-	-
	Introduced grass-shrubland	338	13	0	0	0	0	0	0	0	0	0	0	0
	Introduced forest	37	1	0	0	0	0	0	0	0	0	0	0	0
	Barren and other	487	3	0	0	0	0	0	0	0	0	0	0	0
	all sampled strata	¹33,617	378	202	0.686	0.077	11	0.540	0.835	23,063	2,576	11	18,149	28,055

E.7: Hawai'i, south Kona – survey years 2003, 2009, and 2010

Habitat variable	Stratum	Area (ha)	K	n	Mean density	SE	CV (%)	Lower 95% CI	Upper 95% CI	Mean abundance	SE	CV (%)	Lower 95% CI	Upper 95% CI
Elevation	500-700 m	100	5	0	0	0	0	0	0	0	0	0	0	0
	700-900 m	1,998	17	0	0	0	0	0	0	0	0	0	0	0
	900-1,100 m	2,343	22	0	0	0	0	0	0	0	0	0	0	0
	1,100-1,300 m	2,309	27	2	0.269	0.269	100	0	0.807	621	621	100	0	1,863
	1,300-1,500 m	2,241	42	9	0.506	0.257	51	0.081	1.077	1,133	576	51	181	2,413
	1,500-1,700 m	1,966	65	16	0.499	0.165	33	0.214	0.849	981	324	33	421	1,669
	1,700-1,900 m	944	13	2	0.240	0.224	93	0	0.721	227	211	93	0	680
	1,900-2,100 m	19	0	-	-	-	-	-	-	-	-	-	-	-
	all sampled strata	¹11,901	191	29	0.249	0.079	32	0.118	0.422	2,962	945	32	1,407	5,016
Vegetation	Montane dry-mesic grass-shrubland	238	1	0	0	0	0	0	0	0	0	0	0	0
	Montane mesic forest	4,645	110	27	0.636	0.156	25	0.365	0.963	2,953	725	25	1,695	4,475
	Montane wet forest	1,035	8	2	1.027	0.839	82	0	2.826	1,062	868	82	0	2,925
	Lowland wet-mesic forest	4,368	53	0	0	0	0	0	0	0	0	0	0	0
	Lowland dry-mesic grass-shrubland	93	0	-	-	-	-	-	-	-	-	-	-	-
	Introduced grass-shrubland	163	0	-	-	-	-	-	-	-	-	-	-	-
	Barren and other	1,412	14	0	0	0	0	0	0	0	0	0	0	0
	all sampled strata	¹13,077	191	29	0.307	0.085	28	0.154	0.491	4,015	1,111	28	2,019	6,417

E.8: Hawai'i, central Kona – survey years 2009 and 2010

Habitat variable	Stratum	Area (ha)	K	n	Mean density	SE	CV (%)	Lower 95% CI	Upper 95% CI	Mean abundance	SE	CV (%)	Lower 95% CI	Upper 95% CI
Elevation	500-700 m	11	0	-	-	-	-	-	-	-	-	-	-	-
	700-900 m	1,303	6	0	0	0	0	0	0	0	0	0	0	0
	900-1,100 m	2,947	16	7	0.683	0.309	45	0.190	1.366	2,013	911	45	561	4,026
	1,100-1,300 m	3,473	30	38	2.487	0.498	20	1.585	3.540	8,636	1,729	20	5,503	12,293
	1,300-1,500 m	3,928	37	126	8.825	1.233	14	6.497	11.334	34,664	4,842	14	25,520	44,521
	1,500-1,700 m	3,910	36	157	13.041	1.897	15	9.590	16.700	50,992	7,419	15	37,496	65,296
	1,700-1,900 m	4,369	34	119	11.752	1.446	12	9.015	14.653	51,345	6,316	12	39,388	64,020
	1,900-2,100 m	4,300	0	-	-	-	-	-	-	-	-	-	-	-
	2,100-2,300 m	3,289	30	1	0.052	0.052	101	0	0.156	171	172	101	0	514
	2,300-2,500 m	57	1	0	0	0	0	0	0	0	0	0	0	0
	2,500-2,700 m	0	0	-	-	-	-	-	-	-	-	-	-	-
	all sampled strata	¹23,276	190	448	6.351	0.486	8	5.438	7.365	147,822	11,304	8	126,582	171,422
Vegetation	Montane dry-mesic grass-shrubland	1,160	9	0	0	0	0	0	0	0	0	0	0	0
	Montane dry forest & woodland	3,956	16	1	0.098	0.097	99	0	0.293	386	383	99	0	1,158
	Montane mesic forest	9,423	82	323	11.235	1.042	9	9.364	13.284	105,869	9,817	9	88,233	125,174
	Montane wet forest	3,510	41	107	6.081	1.039	17	4.261	8.401	21,344	3,645	17	14,956	29,487
	Lowland wet-mesic forest	5,747	36	17	0.737	0.198	27	0.347	1.130	4,237	1,137	27	1,994	6,493
	Lowland dry-mesic grass-shrubland	20	0	-	-	-	-	-	-	-	-	-	-	-
	Introduced grass-shrubland	1,489	2	0	0	0	0	0	0	0	0	0	0	0
	Introduced forest	14	0	-	-	-	-	-	-	-	-	-	-	-
	Barren and other	2,320	4	0	0	0	0	0	0	0	0	0	0	0
	all sampled strata	¹27,605	190	448	4.776	0.384	8	4.057	5.563	131,836	10,590	8	111,998	153,561

E.9: Hawai'i, north Kona – survey years 2003, 2009, and 2010

Habitat variable	Stratum	Area (ha)	K	n	Mean density	SE	CV (%)	Lower 95% CI	Upper 95% CI	Mean abundance	SE	CV (%)	Lower 95% CI	Upper 95% CI
Elevation	700-900 m	398	0	-	-	-	-	-	-	-	-	-	-	-
	900-1,100 m	4,017	0	-	-	-	-	-	-	-	-	-	-	-
	1,100-1,300 m	4,969	14	3	0.335	0.238	71	0	0.892	1,663	1,184	71	0	4,433
	1,300-1,500 m	3,696	48	20	1.128	0.471	42	0.405	2.188	4,168	1,742	42	1,496	8,085
	1,500-1,700 m	4,650	87	53	1.829	0.423	23	1.082	2.707	8,504	1,968	23	5,033	12,587
	1,700-1,900 m	4,770	110	60	1.580	0.320	20	1.027	2.254	7,539	1,527	20	4,898	10,754
	1,900-2,100 m	3,136	28	0	0	0	0	0	0	0	0	0	0	0
	2,100-2,300 m	1,588	0	-	-	-	-	-	-	-	-	-	-	-
	2,300-2,500 m	460	0	-	-	-	-	-	-	-	-	-	-	-
	2,500-2,700 m	3	0	-	-	-	-	-	-	-	-	-	-	-
	all sampled strata	¹21,221	287	136	1.031	0.156	15	0.740	1.366	21,873	3,303	15	15,704	28,986
Vegetation	Montane dry-mesic grass-shrubland	1,274	7	0	0	0	0	0	0	0	0	0	0	0
	Montane dry forest & woodland	7,068	121	0	0	0	0	0	0	0	0	0	0	0
	Montane mesic forest	6,467	105	136	3.665	0.457	12	2.807	4.577	23,701	2,955	12	18,154	29,601
	Montane wet forest	1,135	0	-	-	-	-	-	-	-	-	-	-	-
	Lowland wet-mesic forest	5,354	0	-	-	-	-	-	-	-	-	-	-	-
	Lowland dry-mesic grass-shrubland	1,248	39	0	0	0	0	0	0	0	0	0	0	0
	Introduced grass-shrubland	3,998	10	0	0	0	0	0	0	0	0	0	0	0
	Introduced forest	22	0	-	-	-	-	-	-	-	-	-	-	-
	Barren and other	1,085	5	0	0	0	0	0	0	0	0	0	0	0
	all sampled strata	¹21,240	287	136	1.116	0.139	12	0.855	1.394	23,701	2,955	12	18,154	29,601

¹Total excludes unsampled strata areas.

51

Appendix F

Trends in occurrence of 'I'iwi (*Vestiaria coccinea*) by island- or region-specific consistently sampled area (CSA). The quantiles represent subsets of locations (that is, survey stations) at which 'I'iwi were detected, and range in elevation from 0.05 (lowest), 0.50 (median) and 0.95 (highest). The parameter coefficient "intercept" specifies the initial mean elevation (that is, at first year of survey). The coefficient "slope" and associated statistics describe the magnitude and direction of the per-year trend in 'I'iwi occurrence by elevation.

F.1: Kaua'i, interior and exterior

Quantile	Intercept (initial elevation)	Slope	SE	Lower 95% CI	Upper 95% CI	t-value	Pr(>|t|)
0.05	1082	7.00	1.856	5.11	9.83	3.771	0.000
0.10	1136	4.08	1.868	1.37	6.96	2.186	0.029
0.25	1186	3.00	1.039	0.76	4.82	2.886	0.004
0.50	1232	2.60	1.098	0.01	4.58	2.368	0.018
0.75	1305	-0.08	1.659	-2.42	2.58	-0.050	0.960
0.90	1360	-0.75	1.415	-3.64	1.24	-0.530	0.596
0.95	1389	-1.50	0.973	-3.19	0.19	-1.542	0.124

F.2: Maui, northeast

Quantile	Intercept (initial elevation)	Slope	SE	Lower 95% CI	Upper 95% CI	t-value	Pr(>|t|)
0.05	1093	2.50	1.412	0.12	4.06	1.771	0.077
0.10	1162	2.71	1.543	0.42	4.95	1.759	0.079
0.25	1348	1.03	1.515	-0.99	3.61	0.681	0.496
0.50	1587	0.00	1.614	-2.48	2.61	0.000	1.000
0.75	1794	-0.55	1.284	-2.95	1.75	-0.427	0.669
0.90	1974	-1.53	1.717	-4.12	1.60	-0.889	0.374
0.95	2032	0.00	1.124	-2.20	0.41	0.000	1.000

F.3: Maui, southeast

Quantile	Intercept (initial elevation)	Slope	SE	Lower 95% CI	Upper 95% CI	t-value	Pr(>|t|)
0.05	1159	-0.90	1.095	-2.86	0.03	-0.822	0.412
0.10	1188	-0.44	1.004	-1.86	0.35	-0.438	0.661
0.25	1361	-1.68	2.304	-4.28	2.28	-0.731	0.465
0.50	1623	-2.38	1.576	-5.90	0.15	-1.507	0.132
0.75	1877	-5.71	2.066	-9.32	-2.21	-2.766	0.006
0.90	2025	-4.53	1.600	-7.68	-2.33	-2.833	0.005
0.95	2087	-3.58	1.630	-7.72	-0.39	-2.198	0.028

F.4: Hawai'i, Hakalau

Quantile	Intercept (initial elevation)	Slope	SE	Lower 95% CI	Upper 95% CI	t-value	Pr(>|t|)
0.05	1487	-0.15	0.458	-0.64	1.62	-0.321	0.748
0.10	1514	-0.13	0.379	-0.63	0.66	-0.345	0.730
0.25	1582	-0.29	0.454	-1.23	0.80	-0.629	0.529
0.50	1671	-0.29	0.473	-1.50	0.58	-0.604	0.546
0.75	1788	-0.71	0.547	-1.89	0.25	-1.291	0.197
0.90	1871	-0.71	0.481	-1.46	0.09	-1.472	0.141
0.95	1891	-0.35	0.260	-0.63	0.27	-1.366	0.172

F.5: Hawai'i, Keauhou

Quantile	Intercept (initial elevation)	Slope	SE	Lower 95% CI	Upper 95% CI	t-value	Pr(>|t|)
0.05	1592	-0.54	0.399	-1.30	0.08	-1.361	0.174
0.10	1621	-0.62	0.462	-1.36	0.20	-1.338	0.181
0.25	1699	-0.75	0.505	-2.15	0.03	-1.486	0.137
0.50	1750	0.77	0.390	-0.60	1.84	1.973	0.050
0.75	1819	0.00	0.274	-0.81	0.14	0.000	1.000
0.90	1886	-0.69	0.380	-1.13	0.06	-1.823	0.068
0.95	1906	-0.67	0.367	-1.43	0.20	-1.814	0.070

F.6: Hawai'i, Mauna Loa

Quantile	Intercept (initial elevation)	Slope	SE	Lower 95% CI	Upper 95% CI	t-value	Pr(>|t|)
0.05	1544	-1.29	0.727	-1.60	0.08	-1.769	0.078
0.10	1545	0.00	0.764	-0.64	1.28	0.000	1.000
0.25	1560	3.69	2.146	-1.18	5.35	1.720	0.086
0.50	1709	1.67	2.466	-1.76	5.68	0.676	0.499
0.75	1825	-0.75	2.564	-4.31	4.53	-0.293	0.770
0.90	1916	1.64	2.481	-4.30	4.84	0.662	0.508
0.95	1977	0.50	1.673	-1.11	4.06	0.299	0.765

F.7: Hawai'i, central Kona, mid-elevation (1,000–1,500 meters)

Quantile	Intercept (initial elevation)	Slope	SE	Lower 95% CI	Upper 95% CI	t-value	Pr(>|t|)
0.05	1094	0.62	1.458	-0.64	2.82	0.424	0.672
0.10	1159	0.31	1.409	-1.29	1.63	0.218	0.827
0.25	1251	0.50	1.381	-1.52	2.17	0.362	0.718
0.50	1359	-0.23	0.981	-1.95	1.54	-0.232	0.817
0.75	1424	-0.45	0.800	-2.10	1.81	-0.564	0.573
0.90	1464	-0.08	0.742	-1.38	1.42	-0.112	0.911
0.95	1479	0.00	0.537	-0.70	0.46	0.000	1.000

F.8: Hawai'i, central Kona, upper-elevation (greater than or equal to 1,500 meters)

Quantile	Intercept (initial elevation)	Slope	SE	Lower 95% CI	Upper 95% CI	t-value	Pr(>|t|)
0.05	1522	0.00	0.651	-1.23	1.00	0.000	1.000
0.10	1532	0.00	0.763	-1.21	1.34	0.000	1.000
0.25	1596	0.00	0.803	-1.02	1.48	0.000	1.000
0.50	1674	0.29	1.230	-2.58	2.45	0.232	0.816
0.75	1757	0.14	0.886	-1.28	2.25	0.161	0.872
0.90	1809	0.00	0.966	-1.06	1.69	0.000	1.000
0.95	1835	-0.39	0.673	-1.09	0.27	-0.581	0.561

F.9: Hawaiʻi, Puʻu Waʻawaʻa

Quantile	Intercept (initial elevation)	Slope	SE	Lower 95% CI	Upper 95% CI	t-value	Pr(>|t|)
0.05	1388	0.03	1.892	-2.17	2.38	0.017	0.986
0.10	1452	-0.68	2.188	-2.55	3.14	-0.310	0.757
0.25	1525	0.92	2.161	-1.75	4.26	0.427	0.670
0.50	1626	2.24	2.201	-2.19	4.60	1.018	0.311
0.75	1754	1.24	1.585	-2.62	3.63	0.782	0.436
0.90	1837	0.45	1.308	-1.31	1.78	0.345	0.730
0.95	1870	0.00	0.827	-0.32	0.93	0.000	1.000

Appendix G

Estimates of 'I'iwi density used in trend analyses by island- or region-specific consistently sampled area (CSA) (results presented in table 2). Year of survey from which estimates are derived is specified following each island- or region-specific name. Sample size (number of stations sampled) and detections (number of birds observed) are indicated with K and n, respectively. Mean annual density (birds per hectare) are reported with associated standard error (SE), percent coefficient of variation (%CV), and lower and upper 95-percent (95%) confidence intervals (CIs). Locations consisting of just two years of consistently sampled areas, especially using the HFBS data, are included here but not in the mani body of the report.

Island	CSA	Year	K	n	Density	SE	%CV	Lower 95% CI	Upper 95% CI
Kaua'i	interior	1981	140	546	2.798	0.146	5	2.512	3.083
		1989	118	267	3.041	0.190	6	2.668	3.414
		1994	111	110	1.722	0.179	10	1.371	2.072
		2000	193	323	1.702	0.128	8	1.451	1.954
		2005	173	84	0.967	0.111	11	0.750	1.185
		2007	103	68	1.003	0.169	17	0.671	1.335
		2008	173	96	1.093	0.133	12	0.832	1.354
		2012	162	60	0.568	0.090	16	0.391	0.744
	exterior	2000	261	326	1.401	0.123	9	1.160	1.642
		2005	142	72	0.946	0.188	20	0.577	1.315
		2007	104	19	0.298	0.115	39	0.073	0.523
		2008	148	59	0.572	0.114	20	0.349	0.796
		2012	153	30	0.169	0.056	33	0.058	0.279
	both	2000	454	649	1.529	0.004	0	1.521	1.537
		2005	315	156	0.958	0.006	1	0.946	0.969
		2007	207	87	0.649	0.007	1	0.635	0.663
		2008	321	155	0.853	0.005	1	0.843	0.863
		2012	315	90	0.374	0.003	1	0.368	0.380
Maui	northeast	1980	146	175	2.886	0.276	10	2.345	3.425
		1992	146	335	6.401	0.364	6	5.688	7.110
		1993	164	528	8.161	0.365	4	7.446	8.873
		1998	94	251	6.842	0.591	9	5.684	7.993
		1999	96	305	8.283	0.458	6	7.385	9.176
		2000	112	400	9.815	0.498	5	8.840	10.785
		2001	139	460	9.413	0.491	5	8.450	10.371
		2005	111	371	8.348	0.400	5	7.565	9.127
		2012	125	355	8.351	0.627	8	7.122	9.574
	southeast	1980	273	268	2.356	0.198	8	1.968	2.741
		1992	200	421	5.673	0.412	7	4.866	6.476
		1996	56	278	5.091	0.660	13	3.798	6.379
		2001	169	495	5.889	0.434	7	5.039	6.735
		2006	178	401	4.322	0.276	6	3.781	4.860
		2011	184	909	4.056	0.249	6	3.568	4.542

Island	CSA	Year	K	n	Density	SE	%CV	Lower 95% CI	Upper 95% CI
Hawai'i	Hakalau	1977	122	705	10.963	0.777	7	9.440	12.486
		1999	233	1267	13.096	0.624	5	11.873	14.319
		2000	339	2013	14.569	0.526	4	13.537	15.600
		2001	323	1582	11.886	0.460	4	10.984	12.789
		2002	324	1455	10.295	0.425	4	9.461	11.128
		2003	329	1652	11.805	0.540	5	10.748	12.863
		2004	326	1712	12.565	0.524	4	11.537	13.592
		2005	288	1513	12.768	0.601	5	11.589	13.947
		2006	277	1442	12.116	0.568	5	11.004	13.228
		2007	274	1315	9.387	0.450	5	8.504	10.270
		2008	292	1412	11.242	0.528	5	10.208	12.277
		2010	248	1256	12.097	0.749	6	10.629	13.565
		2011	255	1378	11.600	0.636	5	10.354	12.845
		2012	271	1497	12.181	0.664	5	10.880	13.482
	Waiakea	1977	120	263	2.971	0.221	7	2.537	3.405
		2002	118	230	3.627	0.323	9	2.994	4.261
	'Ola'a	1977	70	73	2.044	0.423	21	1.215	2.873
		2010	68	12	0.272	0.112	41	0.051	0.492
	Keauhou	1977	112	315	5.411	0.472	9	4.486	6.336
		1995	244	2272	8.096	0.415	5	7.282	8.911
		1996	117	554	6.879	0.771	11	5.368	8.390
		1997	281	2603	7.045	0.308	4	6.441	7.649
		1998	227	790	6.349	0.434	7	5.498	7.199
		2002	196	701	6.253	0.373	6	5.523	6.984
		2003	204	541	5.124	0.346	7	4.446	5.802
		2005	188	516	4.968	0.350	7	4.281	5.655
		2006	200	488	4.465	0.302	7	3.872	5.058
		2007	199	650	4.688	0.416	9	3.873	5.503
		2008	134	501	6.144	0.527	9	5.111	7.176
		2009	201	557	4.889	0.351	7	4.200	5.577
		2010	213	562	5.458	0.390	7	4.694	6.222
		2011	212	660	6.175	0.436	7	5.320	7.029
		2012	213	481	4.267	0.293	7	3.692	4.841
	Mauna Loa	1978	98	62	1.099	0.246	22	0.617	1.580
		1986	87	46	1.189	0.322	27	0.558	1.819
		1987	85	152	0.838	0.239	28	0.370	1.306
		1990	109	275	1.694	0.403	24	0.903	2.484
		1991	112	219	2.544	0.347	14	1.863	3.224
		1992	125	441	3.130	0.386	12	2.374	3.886
		1993	138	175	1.790	0.253	14	1.294	2.286
		1994	128	230	1.835	0.320	17	1.209	2.462

Island	CSA	Year	K	n	Density	SE	%CV	Lower 95% CI	Upper 95% CI
		2010	77	29	0.635	0.194	31	0.255	1.016
	north Ka'ū	1976	40	69	2.724	0.592	22	1.563	3.885
		2004	75	76	1.436	0.194	13	1.057	1.816
	central Ka'ū	1976	484	433	1.840	0.140	8	1.565	2.114
		2008	238	69	0.586	0.127	22	0.337	0.835
	south Ka'ū	1978	72	20	0.581	0.174	30	0.240	0.922
		2005	51	0	0	0	0	0	0
	south Kona	1978	89	126	2.562	0.423	17	1.732	3.391
		2009	43	5	0.145	0.087	60	-0.026	0.316
	Honomalino	2005	46	21	0.694	0.199	29	0.303	1.085
		2010	43	9	0.416	0.179	43	0.065	0.766
	Central Kona - upper	1978	22	71	3.852	0.720	19	2.441	5.264
		1995	73	133	3.068	0.397	13	2.290	3.847
		1999	71	219	8.536	0.862	10	6.846	10.225
		2000	72	218	9.106	0.984	11	7.177	11.036
		2001	70	237	7.693	0.780	10	6.165	9.222
		2005	73	259	7.555	0.637	8	6.307	8.804
		2006	64	243	10.464	1.296	12	7.923	13.005
		2009	71	339	11.537	1.196	10	9.193	13.880
		2012	72	233	6.488	0.655	10	5.205	7.771
	Central Kona - lower	1978	23	72	5.212	1.217	23	2.828	7.597
		1995	58	117	4.523	0.993	22	2.577	6.469
		1999	79	73	2.433	0.518	21	1.418	3.449
		2000	79	93	2.947	0.607	21	1.757	4.137
		2005	49	88	4.288	0.969	23	2.389	6.187
		2009	73	178	5.179	0.723	14	3.762	6.596
		2012	73	175	4.744	0.558	12	3.650	5.837
	Pu'u Wa'awa'a	1978	32	93	3.958	0.546	14	2.888	5.027
		1990	34	38	2.189	0.578	26	1.056	3.322
		1991	34	46	2.592	0.660	25	1.300	3.885
		1996	33	24	1.320	0.439	33	0.459	2.180
		2003	33	50	4.306	0.967	22	2.411	6.201
		2009	34	52	3.888	0.879	23	2.166	5.611